Ireland's Essential Travel Guide

Discover the best Hotels, Places of interest, malls and night parties for your trip

Table Of Contents

Introduction

If you're the kind of cautious traveler who would rather learn everything about a country first before booking those tickets, then this ebook is the perfect guide for you. It contains enough information on each of the major cities in Ireland that would fill your mind with ease. There are lists of the best places to stay in, pricing information for admission fees on the best places to visit in each city, and a whole lot more.

Even if you never get the chance to book those tickets, reading through this book should be enough to make you feel that you have stepped foot in Ireland. Experience everything that there is to see, feel, and hear about in Ireland without spending anything more than the price you paid for this ebook.

Chapter 1 A Brief History of Ireland

The Early Settlers

Just like many other European nations, Ireland's history dates back to thousands of years ago. Historians have already established the fact that Stone Age farmers came to Ireland in 7000 or 8000 BC. But only recently has it been revealed that these farmers migrated from a region in the Middle East known as the Fertile Crescent. It was originally believed that these migrants came to Ireland and competed for space with the Irish.

However, recent developments have proven that the migrants settled into Ireland and they came to be known as the Irish. So far, there are no traces of any other people living in Ireland before these migrants came. Traces of these early settlements have been found in various locations around Ireland. These include Stone Age tools such as axe-heads and weapons, as well as megalithic tombs that date back to 4000 BC.

Most of the early settlements were located in coastal areas. The people were mostly hunter-gatherers and also took advantage of the sea for their survival. Farming didn't start until 3500 BC when the surrounding forests were cleared for crops. The early settlers also raised cattle.

The Celts

Some historians believe that the Celts came to Ireland at around 500 BC. The Celts were believed to have come in waves. Unlike the early Greek and Roman civilizations, the Celts didn't have an established central community led by one or two rulers. Their communities were scattered around

Ireland. These communities came together every now and then for certain events such as feasts and religious gatherings.

The Celts dominated over the other settlers in Ireland. Their cultures, traditions, and language were copied by the other settlers until it became the dominant lifestyle. The Celts also brought new knowledge with them specifically that of making more refined tools and weapons. But contrary to popular belief, the popular ancient stone monuments in Ireland were not part of Celtic culture.

These monuments already existed before the arrival of the Celts. Continuous archaeological digs have found many traces of Celtic lifestyle all around Ireland, though. Unfortunately, there is no written history at all. That's because the ancient Celts did not trust the written word so relied heavily on their oral traditions. Most of what's written about the Celts was published centuries after they actually happened.

The Celts did have a system of writing known as the Ogham. It was a system of writing that was based on numbers instead of letters. But usage of this writing system was steeped in superstition, which was why it was rarely used. There were a few poets and bards who used it to record events and to write songs and poems. Ogham was also used on tomb inscriptions.

The English

The Normans (British) invaded Ireland at a time when the island already had an established set of rulers. At that time, kings ruled over small kingdoms throughout the island. These kings answered to a High King whose main seat of power was at the Hill of Tara. The Normans invaded England through the request of a disgruntled king, Dermot MacMurragh, the King of Leinster. He had lost his kingdom and needed the Normans' aid in reclaiming it.

Mercenaries that were backed by King Henry II and Pope Adrian IV invaded Ireland in May of 1169. Thus, the tug of war between Ireland and England had begun. The English originally controlled just a small portion of Ireland's eastern region. Through successive invasions and various complex plots, the whole of Ireland soon became a part of the United Kingdom in 1801. But the Irish were rebellious of this status quo.

The Potato Famine did not help matters for England and soon the Irish were once again in revolt. Further upheavals happened before a solution was finally reached to which all concerned parties agreed: the creation of the Irish Free State and the continuation of British control over Northern Ireland. The Irish Free State soon became the Republic of Ireland. It encompasses a large part of the island, measuring around 85% of the total land mass. It is also what people specifically think about when they talk about Ireland in general.

Chapter 2 Language and Climate

Language

Ireland has two official languages: English and Gaelic. Gaelic, also referred to locally as Gaeligh or Irish, is one of the oldest languages in the world that is still being used today. There is no clear evidence of when exactly Gaelic started to be widely used in Ireland. The only thing that historians are certain of is that it has been in use since 2000 to 1200 BC. Archaeological digs have also uncovered Old Irish/Gaelic inscriptions written in the Ogham system.

The English language came to Ireland with the Norman invasion of 1169. From then on, it became the dominant language spoken in the regions that were under English rule. It spread to the Western regions when the British invaded Connaught in 1235. But Gaelic wasn't entirely lost as many of the Irish still spoke the language. For centuries, the British continuously tried to subdue the use of the Irish language.

At one point, speaking Gaelic was even viewed as disloyal to the crown of England. Gaelic also suffered greatly with the loss of many native speakers in the great famine that lasted from 1845 to 1852. When the British finally relinquished its rule, Gaelic was almost non-existent since only 15% of Ireland's total population spoke the language.

In recent years, there has been an active effort from many concerned individuals to bring Gaelic back into popular usage. Despite their best efforts, only a small percentage of the population are currently using it as their first language. But don't be surprised if you see it written in signs or hear traces of it spoken here and there. In fact, many urban speakers have also adapted a form of Hiberno-English. This is a way of incorporating the grammatical style of Gaelic into the usual cadence of the English language.

Climate

Unlike other countries that lie in the same latitude, Ireland experiences mostly mild weather throughout the year. That's because its climate is influenced by the Atlantic Ocean. Rain is quite common in the island and could fall at any time without warning. The summers are generally warm and the winters are quite mild with none of the temperature extremes experienced by other regions.

The seasons fall on the following months:

Spring: February to April. During these months, temperatures could go as high as 54°F.

Summer: May to July, though July and August are considered as the warmest months. During these two months, daylight can last for up to 18 hours per day. Nighttime usually falls at around 11pm. The hottest temperatures are between 64°F and 68°F.

Autumn: August to October. The mildest temperatures are in September.

Winter: November to January. January and February often experience the coldest weather with temperatures dropping to 46°F. However, snow rarely falls even in the coldest days.

Ireland's mild climate makes it an ideal place to visit at any time of the year. Tourists can time their visits to coincide with any of the colorful Irish festivals.

Chapter 3 Dublin

Dublin is the capital city of Ireland and is also one of the oldest in the country. It is also the most populous city with a population count of 1.1 million people as of 2011. The River Liffey cuts the city in half, with each side being referred to as the Northside and the Southside respectively. This division is often the subject of many local jokes and locals could sometimes be passionate about their respective sides.

The government recognizes the year 988 AD as the official founding year of the city. But there is evidence that the settlement may have started as early as 140AD. The city has borne witness to most of Ireland's history. It is located in Leinster, the seat of the very same king who brought about the British invasion of Ireland. As such, Dublin has served a central purpose in most of England's occupancy.

Culture

Just like many capital cities, Dublin is a melting pot of different cultures from different parts of the world. But race or color is never an issue in this city. The locals are quite friendly and are mostly eager to help a tourist with directions at any time of the day. They also love to take advantage of every bit of sunlight that they get by heading off to any of the parks around the city during their lunch breaks whenever it's not raining (a rare occurrence, really).

Tourists who visit the city in time for the St Patrick's festival in March also have to be ready for the heavy crowds in pubs especially after nightfall. Crowds can also be expected in August and September since this is when the finals for the Gaelic Football and a sport called Hurling are held. Fans from all over the country flock to the city to cheer for their favorite teams.

Where to Go

There are numerous sites for tourists to visit in Dublin. Most of these sites are filled with historical importance. They have been preserved throughout the years of Ireland's tumultuous history. But there are also a few noteworthy modern additions to Dublin's famous landmarks. Some of these must-see places include:

1. Kilmainham Gaol – built in 1792, Kilmainham gaol was the place where many Irish revolutionary leaders were sent to die. Ever since it opened, the prison has witnessed the misery of prisoners whose crimes were mostly petty. In fact, the prisoners not only consisted of adult men and women but also of children as young as seven or eight years old who were caught stealing. When the gaol became overcrowded, most of the prisoners were sent to the penal colonies that were established in Australia.

   Kilmainham Gaol is no longer used to house any prisoners today. It has since been converted into a museum through the efforts of the Kilmainham Gaol Restoration Society. Visitors can book guided tours of the gaol at any day of the year.

   Opening times:

   ✦ Opens on Mondays thru Saturdays from 9:30am to 6:00pm during the months of April to September. Last admission is at 5pm.

   ✦ Opens on Mondays thru Saturdays from 9:30am to 5:30pm during the months of October to March. Last admission is at 4:30pm.

   ✦ Opens at 10am and closes at 6pm on Sundays.

   Where to go next: The Irish Museum of Modern Art is just 3 kilometers away on the corner of Emmet Road and Kilmainham Lane. The Guinness Storehouse is just right across the museum.

2. St. Patrick's Cathedral – this is the largest church in all of Ireland. It is also one of the oldest. The parish has been standing since the 12th century and it officially became a cathedral in the early 13th century. It sits beside the well where St Patrick was believed to have converted the pagans when he visited Dublin in 450 AD. Throughout its long history, the cathedral has endured a tug of war in several fronts.

It originally started out as a Catholic establishment but was then converted into the Anglican Church of Ireland after the English Reformation. It briefly reverted back into a Catholic church after repossession by King James II but reverted back to the Anglican faith after his defeat. It has experienced demotion into a regular parish church and then a subsequent promotion back into cathedral status.

The remains of many of its former deans are interred inside the Cathedral. These deans included the famous author Jonathan Swift. His book, Gulliver's Travels, was published 13 years after his election as Dean of the Cathedral. A bust and an epitaph of the famous writer and dean are installed near his burial site inside the cathedral.

St. Patrick's Cathedral is still actively used as a place of worship. Mass schedules are regularly updated on the cathedral's website. Tourists can go sightseeing but would have to pay the admission fee. Adults are normally charged €6 when entering alone. Families with two kids under 16 can pay the group admission fee of €15. Group rates for adults with a minimum of 10 people on the group is at €4.20 each.

Opening times:

+ Guided tours are available on Mondays to Saturdays from 10:30am to 2:30pm.

+ From March to October, the Cathedral opens at 9:30am and closes at 5pm Mondays to Fridays. It opens from 9:00am to 6pm on Saturdays. Sunday opening and closing times are from 9am to 10:30am, 12:30pm to 2:30pm, and 4:30pm to 6pm.

+ From November to February, it has the same opening and closing times on Mondays through Fridays and closes and hour early on Saturdays. Sunday opening and closing times are 9:00am to 10:30am and 12:30pm to 2:30pm only.

Where to go next: Teeling Whiskey Distillery is just an 8-minute walk away at Newmarket Road.

3. Guinness Storehouse – this establishment currently ranks at the top of Europe's list of tourist attractions for 2015. As per its name, the storehouse is dedicated to a drink that has been in Ireland's history since the 1700s. Originally known as the stout porter, the drink was renamed into Guinness in honor of the brewery owner Arthur Guinness.

The seven-storey Guinness Storehouse was opened in the year 2000. It features different aspects of the drink, including its history, its ingredients, the brewing process, and so much more. Its main attraction is the glass atrium that can hold 14.3 million pints of the drink when filled. Visitors can stand at the bottom of the atrium and have their pictures taken from above.

As of 2015, tickets to the storehouse cost €18 and included a free pint of the famous drink. Once tourists are tired of touring the seven-storey facility, they can end their tour in a literally high note. They can head on to the Gravity Bar that's located at the seventh floor. The bar not only serves Ireland's iconic drink, it also provides guests with an unequaled view of the city from all angles.

Opening times:

- ✦ Opens daily from Sundays to Saturdays from 9:30am to 7:00pm.

Where to go next: Christ Church Cathedral and the Dublin Interactive Viking History Museum is only a few blocks away.

4. Dublin Castle or *Caisleán Bhaile Átha Cliath* in Irish – sitting on a total land area of 11 acres, the castle has served different purposes in its long history. The current structure stands on the same ground where King John's castle used to stand. Also known as John Lackland, John was King Henry II's youngest son. As such, there were no English lands left for him to rule hence the surname Lackland. King Henry made him the first Lord of Ireland in 1177 at the age of 10.

The castle continued to serve as the primary seat of the British government in Ireland. When the Irish Free State was formed, the castle was used as a courthouse. Today, the castle is now a government complex that is used for various functions. Most of its rooms have retained its old-world splendor, with decorations that date as far back as the 1700s. The grandest and most important room in the complex is the Saint Patrick's Hall because that's where Ireland's presidents are inaugurated.

Aside from serving as a government complex, the castle now also houses museums and cafés that are accessible to tourists. There are also several parts of the castle that tourists can freely visit. But those who wish to view the State Apartments would have to purchase guided tour tickets. Guided tours are charged at €8.50 per adult and €3.00 for children 6-12 years old. Students and seniors can get a discounted rate of €6.50 provided a valid ID is presented.

Dublin Castle may already be familiar to Hollywood enthusiasts as the Vatican in the popular television series *The Tudors*.

Opening hours:

- ✦ The State Apartments, Chapel Royal, and Medieval Undercroft are open for guided tours on Mondays to Saturdays from 10am to 4:45pm. It opens at 12 noon on Sundays and during Public Holidays and closes at 4:45pm. Guided tours are not available on Good Friday, the 24th to the 28th of December, and the 1st of January.

- ✦ Admission is free to the Chester Beatty Library. It has two schedules:

    - o From the 1st of May to the end of September, it opens on Mondays to Fridays from 10am to 7pm.

    - o From the 1st of October to the end of April, it opens on Tuesdays to Fridays 10am to 7pm.

- ✦ Tourists can play the role of smugglers and tax collectors by visiting the Revenue Museum. It opens on Monday to Fridays from 10am to 4pm.

Where to go next: The Garda Museum is just a stone's throw away.

5. Drimnagh Castle or *Caisleán Dhroimeanaigh* in Irish – this castle is also another familiar sight for Hollywood enthusiasts. That's because it has been the site of several famous Hollywood productions including *Ella Enchanted* and *The Tudors*. The earliest known record of the castle dates back to the early 13th century through the title of ownership under Sir Hugh de Bernival.

The Bernival family, who later came to be known as Barnewell or Barnewall, owned the castle for centuries. Ownership was transferred when Joseph Hatch bought the castle in the 1900s. The castle bears the distinction of being the only remaining castle that still stands in the middle of a moat. Aside from its historical value, the castle is also famous for its picturesque garden.

Opening hours:

- Open on Mondays through Thursdays from 9am to 4pm.

- Opens at 9am on Fridays and closes at 1pm.

- Tourists may be able to book a visit on weekends but they need to set up an appointment first.

Where to go next: Mount Argus Park is just a 12-minute drive away via Kildare Road. If you want to go sightseeing, take the longer route via Sundrive Road. This route takes approximately 24 minutes to traverse.

Those who only get to spend a day in the city can also book a walking tour. Most of these tours cover the most interesting parts of Dublin all in one day, including most of the items listed here. The only disadvantage to a one-day walking tour is that there won't be enough time to explore the insides of each establishment before moving on to the next.

Side trip: If you have enough time, check out the Wicklow Mountain National Park. It covers a large part of the mountain range that's located in County Wicklow, just outside of Dublin. Visiting the park is like going to another world where faeries and nymphs and other woodland creatures abound. There are campsites in the park so visitors can spend more than just a day exploring the heaths and bogs and forestlands of the park.

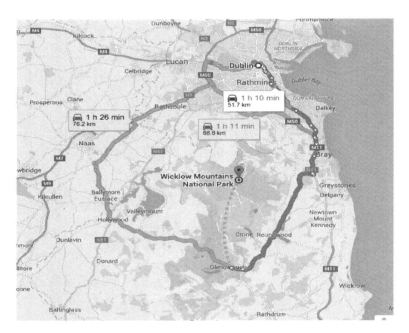

https://www.google.com.ph/maps/dir/Dublin,+Ireland/Wicklow+Moun tains+National+Park,+Laragh,+Co.+Wicklow,+Ireland/

Where to Eat

1. The Lobster Pot – this establishment has been around since 1980. It is located about 2.3miles from the city centre, which is only about 7 minutes of car travel. It is also conveniently located near some of Dublin's popular spots, such as Herbert Park, Landsdowne Road Stadium, and the Royal Dublin Society. The restaurant's menu combines the rich variety of seafood found in the Ireland's seas cooked with a subtle French flair.

    The sumptuous meals are perfectly paired with a wide selection of wines from all over the world. Most of the reviews about this restaurant focus around the homey old-world feel of its cuisine. The restaurant itself also has a cosy ambience, with it brick outside wall, quaint floor-to-ceiling French windows, and an open fireplace. This also makes the restaurant a perfect setting for intimate events such as weddings and the like.

Opening Hours:

- The Lobster Pot is open at dinnertime Monday to Saturdays 6:00pm to 10:30pm. Guests can avail of the Early Bird Set Menu on Mondays between 6:00 and 7:30pm.

- It only opens at lunchtime for guests with prior bookings, and only on Mondays to Fridays.

- Guests can request for an early opening at 5pm whenever there are local events held in the area.

2. Trocadero – this is another one of Dublin's gems. Just like The Lobster Pot, most of Trocadero's staff have been with the restaurant for a long time now. Its current Maitréd started in the kitchen in 1985 and moved up to become co-owner. But the restaurant itself has been around since 1957. This longevity is a testament to the fact that Trocadero offers the best service paired with a delectable menu for a superior dining experience.

The Trocadero offers a mouth-watering menu of traditional Irish food that combines a rich catch from the sea with lamb, chicken, and other seasonal ingredients. Diners can enjoy these exotic offerings amidst an old-world ambience that is reminiscent of the 1950s. The Trocadero also caters mostly to the theatre crowd, which means that its closing hours is dependent on the theatre's hours.

The Maitréd should be able to assist you in choosing the best wine to go with that meal.

Opening hours:

- The Trocadero opens at 4:30pm on Mondays to Fridays and at 4pm on Saturdays.

3. Beaufield Mews – this restaurant has three different settings: Vintage Afternoon Tea, the Loft Brasserie, and

the Coachhouse and Garden. The Vintage Afternoon Tea is held at the restaurant's vintage tea room in honor of its founder, Doreen 'Go-go' Kirwan. This afternoon tea ritual dates back to 1948 when Doreen and her daughters sold pastries and tea while looking for prospective buyers of the Coachhouse's overflowing contents.

The Loft Brasserie has a homey atmophere that brings customers back to the early years of Beaufield Mews. Its location at the upper floor also provides a great view of the estate's courtyard. The glass chandelier and open fire add to the overall sophistication of the place. Not to mention that it also serves sumptuous meals that cater to every palate.

The Coachhouse and Garden serves an award-winning kids' menu that the restaurant is truly proud of. This is the perfect setting for families who want to enjoy some lunch under the Irish sun. Adults can sit back at the Coachhouse and watch the kids play in the adjoining rose garden.

Opening hours:

- Vintage Afternoon Tea is only available on Wednesday to Sunday afternoons, with the last order received at 4pm. Guests would have to book in advance.

- The Loft Brasserie is open on Wednesdays to Saturdays from 6pm onwards. It serves lunch and dinner on Saturdays and Sundays from 12:30pm onwards. Guests do have the option to book a private lunch if they want to.

- The Coachhouse and Garden only serves lunch and opens at 12:30pm.

4. Nancy Hands Bar and Restaurant – this restaurant was established at a time when public (pub) houses where

the 'in' thing in Ireland. The interior furnishings of the place effectively take visitors back to the Victorian Era. The restaurant serves a host of Irish and Scotch whiskys. Guests don't have to worry about their lack of knowledge on the best whisky brands.

That's because the bar offers a demonstration class where guests are educated on the different types of whiskey and which brands are the best of its class. Guests are also given the chance to sample the products.

The restaurant's menu is also quite extensive, with specials that range from stuffed turkey and ham, fresh fish that's coated in a special chilli batter, and a lot more. Nancy Hands also has a selection of bar food for guests who go there mainly to drink.

Opening hours:

- Daily lunch is served Mondays to Fridays 12noon to 3pm.

- The bar is open from 12noon to 11:30pm on Sundays and Mondays and 12noon to 12:30am on Fridays and Saturdays.

5. Brewers' Dining Hall – this is located at the fifth floor of the Guiness Storehouse. This means that guests who arrive at the location without food on their stomachs don't have to go hungry for long. They can enjoy a home-cooked meal at the dining hall while watching the chefs prepare meals through the open kitchen. The restaurant also promotes camaraderie among its guests through its communal dining areas.

Opening hours:

- This follows the same schedule as the storehouse.

Note that all of these restaurants place an emphasis on using locally-sourced ingredients. This includes seafood from Ireland's extensive coastline, free-range poultry products, locally-caught game, and farm-grown herbs, spices, and other produce.

Where to Stay

There's so much for tourists to choose from in terms of accommodation. Those who can afford it can choose to stay in any of the world-class hotels, most of which are located at the city centre. Those who are on a tight budget can also choose to stay in any of the more affordable places. Some of the choices include:

1. Dylan Hotel – this five-star hotel is located in one of Dublin's respectable neighborhoods. Aside from its first-class bedrooms, the Dylan also has a restaurant and bar where guests can chill out. The hotel building is a historic establishment that was founded on the 9th of April 1900 as a nurses' home for the Royal City of Dublin Hospital. Originally, it could only accommodate 30 nurses who each had their own living quarters.

   By the end of the 20th century, the nurses' home and the hospital were sold by its Trust Board to different entities. The hotel has managed to retain the exterior architecture of the building though most of its interior has already been modernized to suit the hotel's needs. The hotel boasts of several signature services such as free wifi, priority upgrades, a dedicated Guest Service Response Team and so on.

   Opening hours:

   + Call +353 1 6603000 or send an email to justask@dylan.ie for inquiries.

2. Ardagh Hotel and Restaurant – this is a popular hotel in the Connemara district. Built on a high location, the Ardagh Hotel provides its guests with an unequalled view of the famous Connemara's sights. It is the perfect hotel to stay in for those who want to have an early start in their Connemara adventures. The Ardagh has been in business for more than 2 decades now.

It also has a restaurant that serves authentic seafood dishes in a background of pink and lavender hues at dinnertime. Some of the hotel's amenities include rooms with great views of the Irish Atlantic coast, parking, and the usual free wifi service.

Opening hours:

- Check-in time is at 3pm and check-out is at 12noon.

- The restaurant normally opens to the public at dinnertime everyday unless otherwise specified.

3. The Latchford Self Catering Apartments – this is one of the choicest self-catering houses in Dublin. It is located in the same impressive neighbourhood as the Dylan Hotel. It is also located right near the homes of some of Dublin's greatest historical figures. This is a perfect choice for families who wish to enjoy their own home-cooked dinners together or to bring home some takeout after a day of adventures.

The Latchford's amenities include a carpark that's open day and night, though it can be accessed through prior arrangements only. Guests can also make use of in-house iron and ironing board at their apartments, cook at the apartment's kitchenette, and dial any number from the Direct Access Telephone. Guests can also request for an external laundry service to take care of their laundry.

Opening hours:

- The Latchford apartments are available for hire all year round. However, since there is a limited number of apartments, it is best to give them a call or shoot them an email first to check for availability. Phone number is +353 (0) 1 6760784 and email ad is info@latchfords.ie.

4. Camac Valley Tourist Caravan and Camping Park – this is a premiere camping site located on Naas Road, approximately 16 kilometres outside of Dublin's city centre. It has won awards from various organizations and is one of the most-recommended sites on tourism review websites. Despite the distance from the city centre, the Camac Valley is actually quite accessible. That's because there is a bus stand situated right outside its front gates.

   Guests can also enjoy a variety of outdoor activities such as fishing, swimming, and golf. Some of the camp's amenities include disabled access, an induction loop for hearing-challenged guests, and a laundry room and kitchenette for campers.

   Opening hours:

   - The camping park is open all year round. Guests can check in at any time. The park normally follows a standard check out time though guests may be able to negotiate a late check-out for an additional fee.

5. Fitzpatrick Castle Hotel – this is one of the most interesting hotels in Dublin. Just imagine living like royalty for a day inside a bona fide castle. The castle was constructed in 1740 and has remained relatively intact since then. But the longevity of the building was not mirrored in its ownership. The castle has changed hands many times from the time it was built.

   The hotel's amenities include tea and/or coffee-making facilities, a hair dryer, a TV, and a trouser press for each room. The pricier suites and executive rooms are also equipped with a workspace with a desk that is suitable for every businessman's needs. The hotel also has a concierge service where guests can arrange for the following:

- ➤ Car rental

- ➤ Hotel chauffeur

- ➤ Pick-up at the airport or the ferry terminal

- ➤ Book restaurants

- ➤ Obtain information about various tours in and outside the city

Guests can also join in any of the fitness classes that are available during their stay. They can also swim some laps on the 20-meter indoor pool or let off some steam at the steam room.

Opening hours:

- ♦ Call +353 1 230 5400 for inquiries on room availability, special offers, and to inquire about check-in and check-out times.

Nightlife in Dublin

Dublin's nightlife consists of a colourful array of music, partygoers, pubs, clubs, and bars, and of course: drinks. It is also a haven for groups who are going on weekend stag and hen parties. Most of these groups are from County Dublin's surrounding areas. There are numerous establishments in the city that cater to various preferences. There are venues that play traditional music, establishments with live bands playing today's popular songs, and clubs that play hiphop and dance songs.

There are also establishments that cater to the more mature set. Dublin's bars and clubs normally start serving drinks at 10 in the morning and stop serving at 11:30pm from Mondays to Thursdays. On Fridays and Saturdays, club-goers can order drinks up to midnight at the latest but only until 11:30pm on Sundays. Those who wish to drink past midnight can go to the late bars. These bars are licensed to serve drinks until 1:30am on weekends.

There are also a number of nightclubs that are licensed to serve drinks until 2:30am.

For a different kind of nightlife, tourists can also book a walking tour that focuses on the spooky side of Dublin. There's also a nighttime tour that gives tourists at least three hours to explore the mountains around Dublin that are known to have a close association with the occult world. This tour is known as the Hellfire Club Tour and is part of the Hidden Dublin Walks tour packages.

Another wholesome night-time entertainment option in Dublin is to listen to some of the best modern poets go on a gabfest of spoken-word poetry. Their usual haunts include Brogan's Bar where they compete with each other on Tuesday nights for the Write & Recite competition. Another haunt for these spoken-word artists is the Stag's Head pub where a monthly pop-up competition is held for poets, musicians, and comedians.

Chapter 4 Cork

Cork is the second most populous city in Ireland with a population of 190,384 as of the 2011 census. It is often considered by locals as the second most important city in Ireland next to Dublin. The metropolitan area of Cork that encompasses various towns and suburbs has a combined total population of more than 300,00 people. Cork's city centre is situated on an island in the middle of the River Lee.

Cork also has a long history and not all of it was spent under British rule. Cork's founder is believed to be Saint Finbarr, the city's patron saint. He founded a monastery on the island in the 6th century. The Vikings arrived sometime around 820-846 AD and created a trading port in the area. The fact that the Viking settlement and the monastery was able to coexist in relative peace is still a surprise to many historians.

Under British rule, Cork played a role in the War of the Roses when it sided with the Yorks. The major players of that rebellion were executed after a failed plot against King Henry VII's rule. Cork also played a major role in the War of Independence, advocating for Irish Home Rule and subsequently standing firm behind William O'Brien.

Culture

The population of Cork consist of an eclectic mix of races though it is predominantly Irish. This mix of races means that Cork also has several establishments that are dedicated to providing services from each race's home country. There are Chinese, Filipino, Jewish, French, Polish, Lithuanian, and Thai restaurants and cafes. There are synagogues, temples, mosques, churches in almost every nook and cranny.

Cork has several art schools and theatre companies that boast some famous Hollywood names as its products, including the dashing Cillian Murphy.

All of these combine to make Cork an exciting city for any tourist to explore. Not to mention that it can also serve as a good starting point for exploring the stone circles and ancient monuments that are abundant in County Cork.

Where to go

1. Skibberreen Heritage Centre – the Great Famine plays a major role in Irish history. It greatly diminished Ireland's population not just through the death of impoverished families but also through outward migration. Tourists who want to truly understand the impact of the famine can visit the Skibberreen Heritage Centre. But the Great Famine is not the only reason for visiting the centre.

   Tourists can also enjoy the great outdoors through the Lough Hyne Marine Nature Reserve. This is the first of its kind in Ireland. The reserve is also unique because it is situated within a marine lake that receives seawater through a narrow channel. The lake has been extensively studied ever since marine biologists first discovered its presence in 1886.

   As such, the Marine Reserve has a hundred years' worth of photo documentation. Tourists can view these photos by buying the coffee table book from the Heritage Centre's official website. Aside from visiting the lake, tourists can also walk along the Knockomagh Wood Nature Trail. The trail takes them to several important sites in the area, such as the holy wells Tobarín Súl and Skour. The trail also provides a great view of the ruins the O'Driscoll's castle on Castle Island, as well as the ruins of St. Brigit's church.

   Opening hours:

- The Heritage Centre is open during the months of March to November only. The schedule also varies as follows:

  o The 18th of March to 19th of May and 28th of September to the 31st of October: open on Tuesdays to Saturdays from 10am to 6pm.

  o The 22nd of May to the 27th of September: open on Mondays to Saturdays 10am to 6pm.

- Tourists need to set an appointment from Mondays to Fridays before they can visit the Centre from the 1st to the 21st of November.

- The centre is closed on the remaining days of November through February.

Where to go next: Skibbereen is a small town surrounded by vast tracts of farmland. After the visit to the Heritage Centre, you may as well go for a drive and take some amazing photos of the Irish countryside. Don't forget to stop over at the picturesque view at the edge of the Coronea Industrial Estate. The Skibbereen Cathedral is also located near the Heritage Centre.

2. Knockdrum Stone Fort – this circular stone fort lies on top of a hill that is located about 83.8 kilometers away from the city of Cork. The fort is believed to have been the home of a high-ranking family during the Bronze Age. Its location provides an uninterrupted view of the sea and its surrounding islands. Today, this uninterrupted view would most certainly be appreciated by weary tourists who are in a meditative mood. It also serves as a great backdrop for those drool-worthy social media posts.

The view also encompasses the Garranes Fingers, also known as the Three Fingers. These are three stones of varying heights aligned in an ENE-WSW direction. It is possible to get a closer look at these stones, but visitors would have to gain permission from the land owner first as it sits on private property.

While on the fort, visitors might also be interested in exploring its sou-terrain to see if the legend is true: that this underground passage leads to a lake situated nearby. If the endeavor fails, then they can just be content with taking great photos around the fort. A good number of artefacts have been deposited on the fort for safekeeping by the amateur archaeologist Boyle Somerville.

Opening hours:

+ Anytime you feel fit enough to climb the 90 or so steps up towards the fort. It doesn't have fixed opening or closing hours and is open for everyone to explore.

Where to go next: Head over to Castletownshend and go whale watching at the marina or sign up at the Cork Whale Watch center to hire a boat. Don't forget to stop over at the Drishane House, Gardens and Museum on the way to or from the whale watching expedition. The Dirshane House is a memorial to Edith Somerville, the famous Irish novelist of the late 1800s.

3. Kealkill Stone Circle – this is located in the small village of Kealkill in West Cork. The village is about an hour's ride from Cork City covering a distance of about 73.5 kilometers. This stone monument is valuable for archaeologists because of the rare and mysterious radial stone cairn. Experts believe that the monument was used by the ancient Irish to observe the complete lunar cycle.

This is a justifiable observation since the monument is located on a spot where the view is unobstructed for miles on all sides. This view is something that tourists who visit the site would definitely be able to take advantage of for their regular social media updates.

After checking the stone circle, explore the quaint village of Kealkill and bask in its quiet small town warmth.

Opening hours:

+ Tourists can visit the site at any time of the day. There are no entrance fees or closed gates to worry about. They just need to make sure that they're fit enough to do a little bit of climbing to the top of the mountain.

Where to go next: Don't forget to check out the ruins of the Carriganass Castle in the outskirts of the village. The castle dates back to the 16th century and once belonged to the powerful O'Sullivan clan.

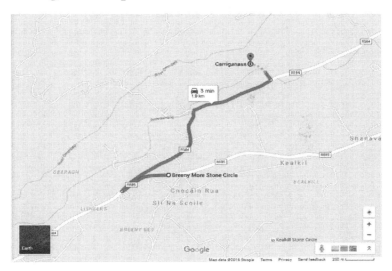

https://www.google.com.ph/maps/dir/Breeny+More+Stone+Circle,+Kealkill,+Co.+Cork,+Ireland/Carriganass,+Cork,+Ireland/

4. Youghal Heritage Town - Youghal is a tiny resort town that's located 52.3 kilometers from Cork City. The town

has managed to retain most of its historical sites, which is why it's referred to as a heritage town. The town's name is believed to have come from the Old Irish term for the yew woods or *Eochaill* that used to dominate the area. Before falling into British hands, Youghal was a Viking settlement. Traces of Neolithic habitation have also been found in the area.

Opening hours:

+ The entire town is the heritage site. This means that there are plenty of places to see. It also means that opening and closing hours may vary depending on the establishment. It is best to just go to the town and explore its wonders from morning to evening.

Where to go next: Head over to Leahy's Open Farm in Dungourney. Travel time takes more or less 30 minutes through three different routes. The entire family would certainly enjoy bonding with the farm animals. There are also a number of outdoor activities to enjoy around the farm, such as going on adventure trails and exploring the farm's museum. Visitors also get to see a real well-maintained Viking Crannog (dwelling place).

5. Blarney Castle – Ireland is dotted with medieval castles that each tells its own story. Blarney Castle is one of the most interesting castles not only because of its medieval architecture. It is also visited by tourists and locals because it holds the magical Blarney Stone, better known as the Stone of Eloquence. Legend has it that when people kissed the stone, they were gifted with the skill for eloquence. There are many stories that surround the stone's origins depending on who's telling the tales.

The only thing that historians are certain of is that the stone was set into the castle's fortifications by Cormac

MacCarthy. MacCarthy served as the King of Munster in the early 14th century. The MacCarthy family owned the castle until the 1690s when it was confiscated by Williamites after defeating the 4th Earl of Clancarty. The castle is currently owned by the Colthurst family.

Opening hours:

The castle and its gardens are open to visitors from Mondays to Saturdays the whole year round. However, closing times vary depending on the month. The schedules are as follows:

- January to February: 9:00am to 5:00pm

- March to April: 9:00am to 6:00pm

- May: 9:00am to 6:30pm

- June to August: 9:00am to 7:00pm

- September: 9:00am to 6:30pm

- October: 9:00am to 6:00pm

- November to December: 9:00am to 5:00pm

Last admission is normally 30 minutes prior to the closing time.

Where to go next: Head over to the Blarney Woollen Mills to shop for some of the finest Irish products. These include personalized Celtic jewelry, capes and shawls sewn in the unique Irish way, and other forms of memorabilia. This is the best place to buy souvenirs of your time in Ireland.

Side trip: The Beara Peninsula at the south-western tip of County Cork is a good place to go to even if it's not part of your itinerary. There are a lot of activities that can be done in the area. The most popular one is to traverse the Ring of Beara, a driving route that takes you in a circular pattern around the peninsula. It is the best way to see some of the best sights that the Beara Peninsula has to offer.

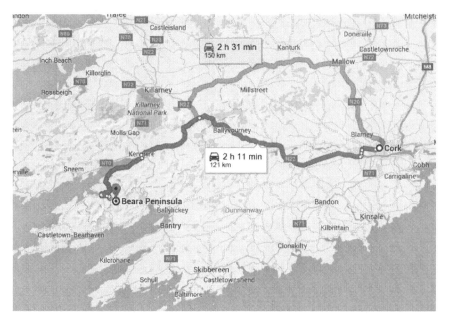

https://www.google.com.ph/maps/dir/Cork,+Ireland/Beara+Peninsula/

Where to Eat

1. The Church Restaurant – this quaint restaurant is located in Skibbereen and offers diners a lot more than just food. Its name is derived from the fact that the building served as a Methodist church since 1833. Church services stopped in 2003 and the building was carefully restored and converted into a restaurant in 2005. After its initial restoration, most of the church's original furnishings were maintained.

Unfortunately, a huge fire destroyed everything except for a two cast iron column, the front doors, and a marble plaque. The restaurant serves breakfast, lunch, and dinner, as well as desserts. The menu includes traditional Irish dishes with ingredients that are 100%

Irish as well. The meat, seafood, vegetables, and other produce are all sourced from local Irish vendors.

Opening hours:

- The restaurant opens at 9am and closes at 6pm on Mondays to Thursdays.

- It closes at 9:00pm on Fridays and Saturdays with the same opening time.

- It opens at 12:30am and closes at 8:00pm on Sundays.

2. Mary Anne's Bar and Restaurant – this is one of the oldest pubs in Castletownshend, having been around since 1846. Its current owners have skillfully maintained its old-world charm by doing constant repairs. Mementos of the past are also apparent in the restaurant's interior. The building is split between a dining room in the upper level and a bar out back. The bar is often booked by locals for private events, so don't be surprised if you're not admitted there on your visit.

Outdoor dining regardless of the weather is made possible by retractable awnings that fit perfectly over the tables. The restaurant's menu is a mixture of traditional Irish dishes and Asian-inspired recipes. Special menus are offered for special holidays. It provides a welcome retreat after a tiring day spent exploring the ruins of Knockdrum.

Opening hours:

- Mary Anne's is open all week (Mondays to Sundays) from 11:00am to 9:00pm.

3. O'Connor's Seafood Restaurant – tourists who have had enough of the mountainous regions of Kealkill can head over to Bantry for a change of scenery. It's only a 12-minute drive through R584. O'Connor's superb seafood dishes make the travel from Kealkill well worth it. Their

menu items regularly changes according to the availability of prime seafood products.

Opening hours:

- ⚓ O'Connor's opens daily from 12 noon and closes after dinnertime.

4. The Walter Raleigh Hotel Restaurant – the historic Walter Raleigh Hotel is home to three fine dining restaurants: The River Restaurant, The Walter, and The Blackwater Restaurant. Each restaurant has its own distinct charm. The River Restaurant provides a brasserie-style dining experience. Its name is derived from the River Blackwater that can clearly be seen from its windows.

The Walter has more of an old-world gentleman's club charm with its brown wood furnishings and open fire. The Blackwater is a stylish breakfast room that provides early risers with a great view of the sea.

Opening hours:

- ⚓ Guests are advised to check with the reception to determine each restaurant's opening times.

5. The Square Table – the menu selections in this restaurant contain ingredients that bear some sentimental value for the owner. Specifically, most of the ingredients are based on the ingredients that the owners' mother always used. The owners are twins Martina (the chef) and Tricia (the manager) Cronin. The restaurant's menu includes home-baked sandwiches, smoked salmon with Irish crab, and a lot more. The restaurant also has an extensive wine list suitable for each of their trademark dishes.

The sisters aim to make the restaurant a leading fine dining establishment that does not come with the usual strings attached to fine dining.

Opening hours:

- ⚜ The Square Table opens daily for lunch and dinner.

Where to Stay

1. Celtic Ross Hotel – this hotel is located in Rosscarberry, just 19 minutes away from the Skibbereen Heritage Centre via the N71. Once you're done exploring the village, head on over to the Celtic Ross Hotel to recharge for the night. In the morning, go out and explore this part of Ireland's popular Wild Atlantic Way with its beaches, cliffs, watchtowers, and an all-encompassing view of the Atlantic Ocean.

   The hotel is located at the edge of Rosscarberry on top of a cliff that overlooks the bay. The rounded turret on side of the building adds to the hotel's otherworldly charm. Most of its rooms, as well as its public places, provide great views of the bay. Aside from providing first-class accommodation and a sumptuous dining experience, the hotel also has a spa and a 15-meter swimming pool. Guests don't have to endure the chill of the bay's waters just to go for a morning swim.

   Other hotel amenities include a bubble pool, a fully-equipped gym, and exercise classes for interested participants.

   Opening hours:

   - ⚜ The Hotel's Leisure Centre opens at 7:30am to 10:00pm Mondays to Fridays and 9:00am to 8:00pm on weekends and bank holidays. The pool is closed when swimming lessons are ongoing and for few days during Christmas.

+ Check-in and check-out is typically the same as that of other hotels in the area, though it's best to confirm this with reception.

2. The Castle Townshend – no, this accommodation's name is not just a clever wordplay on the name of village where it's located. It's actually the real thing: a Castle named Townshend. The castle's name, and subsequently the entire village's name, was derived from the Townshend family name. Richard Townshend had the castle erected in 1650. Ownership remains with his family to this day and some of his descendants still reside in the castle.

Castle Townshend provides two different accommodation options: self-catering apartments and Bed and Breakfast rooms. The B&B rooms are guest bedrooms within the castle. All the rooms are equipped with its own toilet and bath but not all of it has a view of the sea. Just imagine the novelty of living in a real 17th-century castle and having free rein to explore its grounds.

The self-catering apartments include three cottages located in the castle grounds and a 5-bedroom house in the castle's courtyard. There is also one self-contained bedroom inside the Castle's tower. These are mostly let out to holiday-goers in groups of 2 to 6.

Opening hours:

+ Check in time for both the self-catering apartments and the b&b rooms is between 3 and 6pm. Check out time is at 11am.

3. Seaview House Hotel – this is a hotel that's set as a country house located in the charming village of Ballylickey. The proprietor, Kathleen O'Sullivan, has been running the hotel for three decades now. In all those years, the hotel has bagged several awards from various award-giving bodies in the hospitality industry.

It is conveniently located just 4 minutes away from the famed Ballylickey Bridge. It also just 6 minutes away from the village of Kealkill via R584.

The hotel can serve as a good base for exploring the rugged coastline of West Cork and its equally stunning countryside. The hotel's facilities include a TV in each of the rooms, as well as toiletries including a hairdryer, and a telephone. Guests can request for either a tea or coffee-making service to be made available in their rooms.

Opening hours:

- Give the hotel a call at +353 27 50073 / 50462 or send an email to info@seaviewhousehotel.com to verify check-in and check-out times.

4. Quality Hotel and Leisure Center – this hotel is located along the banks of Redbarn Beach, about an hour's ride from the historic town of Youghal. But the travel is worth it because the hotel provides a great view of the sea from most of its rooms. It is also a good place for couples to have some quiet time together and enjoy a quiet sunset stroll. Youghal is a resort town so there should be plenty of beaches there too, but these could become overpopulated.

On the other hand, Redbarn Beach has a more private feel to it. Guests can choose between the hotel's self-catering apartments and its hotel bedrooms. The hotel also has a selection of fitness and leisure activities that guests can take part in. These include a children's play pool, a gym, a spa, and a 20-meter heated swimming pool.

The hotel's in-room amenities also include a TV on each of the rooms and a DVD player. There is also a mini fridge, free wifi service everywhere in the hotel, and a tea and coffee-making facility. The entire hotel also provides access for wheelchairs.

Opening hours:

- Just call the hotel at +353 023 88 36400 or send an email to info.clonakilty@qualityhotels.ie for inquiries on opening times and room availability.

5. Blarney Castle Hotel – this hotel is located just a minute away from Blarney Castle, which is where it got its name. The hotel was established in 1837 and prides itself with welcoming guests in a traditionally Irish way: with an open fire and lots of friendly smiles. Guests are also treated to a concert of traditional music at the hotel's bar.

The hotel's amenities include en-suite toilet and bath, free wifi, separate cots for young children, and a wake-up call by request. It is also a good base for exploring the village of Blarney through scenic walks, bike rides, and horseback riding.

Opening hours:

- Music playing starts at 9:30pm on Mondays, Tuesdays and Thursdays. The bar only plays music that starts at 8:00pm on Wednesdays during the summer season only.

Nightlife in Cork

Those who are interested in wholesome nighttime pursuits can visit the Cork Opera House at any time. That would help give them a better understanding of why ballet is an intrinsic part of every Irish citizen's life. The opera house can seat up to 1,000 guests and it has a wide selection of events that guests can choose to watch. Some of the shows lined up for the month of April include the opera version of Dangerous Liaisons and a show by acclaimed artists Paul Heaton and Jacqui Abbott. Shows at the opera normally start at around 7pm onwards.

The theatre is another wholesome form of entertainment in Cork. The city has three different theatres that each present different shows every night. The Cork Arts Theatre is the most popular among the three and is also the hub where many of Cork's leading artists go for some tete-a-tete. These establishments are also often surrounded by pubs that are dedicated to the theatre crowd. This means that they open and close according to the theatre's opening and closing times.

But if you really want to experience getting drunk in Cork, then there is a long list of places to go to all around the city. Bodega is a must-visit night spot because it provides a nice mixture of entertainment and art through the displayed works of Irish artist Jack Butler Yeats. The SoHo bar is also another favorite haunting ground for Cork's local populace. It is big and spacious and is the place to be for those who want to catch some of the local gossip.

Other notable bars and clubs in Cork City include the Long Valley Bar, the Bowery, the Hanover, and the Voodoo Rooms. The latter has been popular from the moment it opened in 2014 to this day. That's probably because it is one of the few clubs in Cork that boasts lasers and disco balls scattered about the room with a live DJ spinning tunes the whole night.

Those who prefer to enjoy some live traditional Irish music can go to the Sin È (shin ay). The name of the place literally means 'that's it', which is humorous reference to the Sin È's next-door neighbour: a funeral parlour. Another unique destination for some live music is the Kino concert venue. It is the establishment that provides live music without serving any alcoholic drinks of any kind. Aside from live music, guests can also take part in film screenings and theatre shows at the Kino.

Chapter 5 Limerick

Frank McCourt made Limerick famous the world over thanks to his autobiographical novel, Angela's Ashes. The book is about his life as a child and teenager in Limerick. One thing that his readers probably came to be familiar with was the fact that it was always raining in Limerick. Through McCourt's books, readers also became familiar with the misery of the poor people in Limerick in the early to mid-1900s.

But that should not be the image that sticks to everyone's minds, because there's more to Limerick than what's written in one book. The earliest recorded history of Limerick was that of a Viking settlement in 812 AD on King's Island. However, there are traces in other historical records that a settlement may already have existed in the island at around 150AD. There is also evidence that St. Patrick went to the island in 434 to baptise a king by the name of Carthann the Fair.

The Vikings invaded in 812. The Normans then followed in the late 12th century. It was they who built the historic buildings that helped redefine Limerick's landscape. Most of these buildings are still standing to this day. But the British also brought a lot of turmoil to the city with all their wars and power struggles. When peace came in the 18th century, Limerick prospered thanks to its bustling port. Soon the railway opened and connected Limerick to other cities, specifically to Dublin and Cork.

Culture

Limerick was named Ireland's National City of Culture in 2104 due to the abundance of artistic and cultural festivals in the city. Irish art that date back to the 18th century is permanently displayed at the Limerick City Gallery of Art. Limerick is also home to several theatre companies and has a bustling music scene. Aside from McCourt, other native Limerickmen and women include the popular 90s band The Cranberries.

Where to go

1. Limerick's Museums – first on the list is the Frank McCourt Museum, of course. The museum was established in the same building as Leamy's school on Harstonge Street. It contains memorabilia of Frank McCourt's life, including a bust of the author at front lawn. The museum also reconstrucst most of the scenes from Angela's Ashes, including the classroom where Frank spent most of his school years.

   From the Frank McCourt museum, they can proceed to the Hunt Museum on Rutland Street. It contains a vast collection of ancient artefacts from some of the oldest civilisations in the world. This includes a collection from the Olmec Civilization, an ancient civilization that existed even before the Mayan and Aztec Civilizations.

   Other museums within the city are The Masonic Centre on Castle Street, Thomond Park Museum, and the Limerick Museum at the Merchant's Quay.

   Opening hours:

   + The Frank McCourt museum opens at 11:00am and closes at 4:30pm on Mondays to Fridays. Visitors need to have a prior appointment when visiting on weekends. Call +353 (61)319710 to inquire about admission fees and tour packages.

   + The Hunt Museum is open from 10am to 5pm Mondays to Saturdays and 2pm to 5pm on Sundays and Bank Holidays. Adults are charged €5.00 while children are charged €2.50. Families may be able to take advantage of the family tour fee of €12.00.

⁜ Thomond museum opens at 9:30am on Mondays to Fridays. Visitors are advised to book a guided tour beforehand though this is not required on weekdays. Pre-booking is necessary for weekend tours, though. Visitors also have the option to buy tickets for the museum only or to include a tour of the Thomond Stadium as well. A tour of the museum and stadium can be booked for €10.00 per adult, €7.00 for seniors, and €8.00 for children aged 6 to 16 years old.

⁜ The Limerick City Museum is open from 10am to 1pm and 2 to 5 pm Mondays to Fridays. Admission is free for all ages.

Where to go next: After stuffing yourself with Irish history, head on out of Limerick to Doon Lough in County Clare. It is a Natural Heritage Area that's approximately 27 minutes away from the city by car.

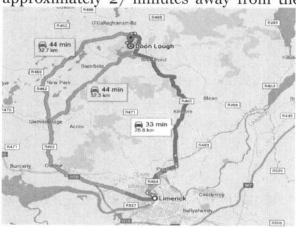

https://www.google.com.ph/maps/dir/Limerick,+Ireland/Doon+Lough/

2. Lough Gur or *Loch Gair* Prehistoric Site – lying 21 kilometers away from the city, Lough Gur has witnessed the ebbs and flows of human life for more than 6000 years. The area was first settled by Stone Age people until more and more people came and developed it until the post-medieval period. It bears the marks of ancient

Irish history through the scattering of stone circles, Neolithic dwelling places, crannogs (fortified dwelling), castles, and megalithic tombs. These ancient sites create a magical quality to the area that is enhanced by the placid beauty of the lake.

The site is run by the Lough Gur Heritage Centre and managed by a group of volunteers known as the Lough Gur Development. These volunteers are also responsible for managing the different festivals and events that commemorate the ancient history of the lake and its surrounds.

Opening hours:

- Guided and Group tours of Lough Gur can be booked through the Heritage Centre. The centre's schedule varies depending on the month. The schedule is as follows:

  - March 27 to October 30:

    - Mondays to Fridays 10:00am to 5:00pm

    - Saturdays, Sundays, and Bank Holidays 12noon to 4:00pm

  - October 31 to March 26:

    - Mondays to Fridays 10:00am to 4:00pm

    - Saturdays, Sundays and Bank Holidays 12noon to 4:00pm

Note that this schedule does not include the period from the 23rd of November to the 26th of December as the site is closed to visitors.

Where to go next: Head over to the town of Kilmallock, which is about 16 to 19 kilometers from the lake. The distance depends on which route you take. Let the village tell its story, as it is also filled with traces of Ireland's long history.

3. King John's Castle or *Caisleán Luimnigh* – the castle was built on King's Island in 1200 on King John's orders. This was the same site where the old Viking settlement in Limerick used to stand. Most of the castle has remained intact through the centuries. In the early 1900s, a team of archaeologists excavated one part of the castle. They uncovered the remains of the Viking settlement.

The last known leader of the settlement was Domhnall Mór Ó Briain. Ó Briain burned the city to the ground in an attempt to prevent the Normans from capturing it. Unfortunately, it still fell under Norman hands when the Vikings were defeated.

The castle was built as a fortress for guarding against the Gaelic kingdoms of western Limerick. It also served to keep any rebellious Norman Lords at bay. It helped ensure the prosperity of the city as an important trading port. The castle underwent 5 different siege attempts in the mid- to late-17th century. In 1641, it also served as a hiding place for Protestants who were escaping the Irish rebellion.

The castle underwent extensive repair and redevelopment in 2013. It now serves as a museum that displays Limerick's rich heritage.

Opening hours:

- The castle opens to visitors at 9:30am every day of the year. It closes at 5:30pm during the months of April to September, and 4:30pm from October to March. It is closed on the 24th to the 26th of December.

Where to go next: Take a tour of the entire King's Island since it is the most historic part of Limerick. There are many other historic buildings on the island, including St Mary's Cathedral, the Old Bishop's Palace, and the ancient walled city known as Englishtown.

4. Glenstal Abbey – located 16.3 kilometeres from Limerick, this Benedictine monastery lies on 500 acres of land far from the noise of the city. Aside from the monastery, the estate also includes a boys' boarding school and a farm. There is a 12-room guest house where guests can stay overnight. The abbey also provides home-cooked meals to all guests.

There is no standard rate of fees for staying at the abbey and guests are given the option to offer donations of any amount. Guests can also join the monks in prayer and are free to roam around the front and back gardens. This is the perfect spot for couples who wish to spend some alone time or single people who need time for meditation.

Guests who wish to be alone for a longer period can book a minimum of 3 nights stay at any of the God pods scattered along the grounds. These pods are completely cut off from civilization, with no wireless internet service at all. The pods are equipped with modern amenities such as a fridge, microwave oven, and electric hob. Unlike the guest house, the pods do have a minimum amount for donation, which is at €40 for 3 nights.

Opening hours:

+ Check in time for the guest house is at 2:00 to 5:00pm daily. Check out time is at 11:00am of the following day.

+ The check in time for the God pods is from 2:00pm to 4:00pm and the check out time is also 11am.

Where to go next: After enjoying some me-time at the Abbey, head back out to the city to enjoy more of its sights. Check out the Bunratty Castle and Folk Park first, located along the corner of Limerick and Ennis Road. A daytime tour of the park is enough to satisfy any avid explorer. The park normally opens at 9am and closes at 5:30pm every day throughout the year.

5. Ballyhoura Mountains – this mountain range lies between two counties: County Cork and County Limerick. It encompasses several towns and villages from both sides. Tourists who want to visit the mountains are advised to reserve at least 2 days on their itinerary for the entire experience. There's so much to do and see in Ballyhoura. But the most popular activity for both locals and tourists is exploring the Ballyhoura Mountain Bike Trails.

The trail extends for 98 kilometers, the longest of its kind in Ireland. The trail consists of several loops with various starting points. These loops take bikers to some of the most picturesque places over rolling hills and flowing streams. There are also several high points on the trail that provide great views of the surrounding countryside. At some point, bikers may also stop over at some of the other previously-listed sites such as the Neolithic structures in Lough Gur.

Opening hours:

- The trail's carpark is open on Mondays to Fridays from 8:00am to 9:00pm and Saturdays and Sundays 8:00am to 8:00pm.

Where to go next: Explore the town of Newcastle West that lies right in the middle of County Limerick. This is the second largest town in the county after Limerick City. The ruins of a 13th-century castle lies at the center of the town, which is fitting since the town of Newcastle grew around that castle in medieval times.

The town is also believed to have served as a battleground where many of the Knights Templar lost their lives.

Side trip: Go on a sightseeing trip of County Clare, which lies on the other side of the River Shannon. Spend a day or two exploring its Neolithic stone monuments, the ruins, and the traces of medieval history that can be found in many of its towns. Note also that the world-famous Cliffs of Moher is in County Clare. If you haven't been there yet, then now is probably the best time to visit.

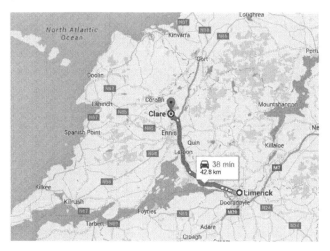

https://www.google.com.ph/maps/dir/Limerick,+Ireland/Clare,+Co.+Clare,+Ireland/

Where to Eat

1. McGettigan's Pub – this restaurant has branches not only in parts of Ireland, but in many countries all over the world. Its Limerick branch was opened in 2014. It is a perfect spot for tourists who are also sports enthusiasts. That's because McGettigan's shows live coverage of sporting events throughout the day. The Pub also plays some live music from a selection of local Limerick artists such as Pa O Donnell, Phil in the Blanks, Tiny Giants, and a lot more.

Their menu focuses on traditional Irish food and includes many of their signature dishes that are loved all over the world. The ingredients are all locally-sourced, which ensures the freshness and quality of the produce.

Opening hours:

- 4 Tourists can order a Full Irish breakfast at the restaurant starting at 10:30am all the days of the week. Closing time on Sundays to Thursdays is at 11:30pm. They stay open for one more hour on Fridays and Saturdays and close at 12:30am.

2. Vines Grill and Wine Bar – the restaurant is located inside the Ballyneety Golf Club and is just 10 kilometers away from the city centre. It offers diners the luxury of enjoying their meals in a relaxed setting and with a great view of greenery for miles. The menu is divided into several categories such as Light Bites, Golfers, Children, and A La Carte. The entries in all of these menus are all sourced locally.

The ingredients for their seafood menus are all sourced from the popular seafood distributor, O'Connell's, in West Cork. The Vines is a favorite among Limerick's local communities as a place where special occasions are celebrated. They go there to celebrate Confirmations, First Communions, and Weddings, or to simply catch up on the events of the week.

Opening hours:

- 4 The restaurant is open all week.

3. The Curragower Bar and Restaurant – the River Shannon serves as the magnificent backdrop for this restaurant. That's because the Curragower sits right on its banks. The restaurant is popular among locals because its food selection tastes beyond delicious. A testament to this is the fact that the Curragower's

menus have consistently been winning awards and honors from various award-winning bodies throughout the years.

When visiting the Curragower's, try to request for an outdoor table to get a better view of the surrounding sights. This view includes King John's Castle, the City Hall, and of course the River Shannon.

Opening hours:

+ The Curragower opens at 12:30pm on Mondays to Thursdays and 12noon on Fridays to Sundays. Food service is only until after dinner at 8:00pm though guests can still stay for drinks at the bar until late.

4. The Locke Bar and Restaurant – this restaurant is also conveniently located near Limerick city's medieval attractions, including King John's Castle. The Locke is a traditional Irish pub where guests get to delve into everything that's great about Irish tradition. That includes the famed Irish hospitality, as well as the lively Irish music. Not only that, the Locke also has quite an extensive menu that offers different kinds of dishes to match every type of palate.

The Locke's interiors are also furnished in a traditionally Irish way that is reminiscent of Irish pubs of the mid- to late-1900s. It also has a huge beer garden for guests who wish to dine *al fresco*.

Opening hours:

+ The Locke opens at 9:00am on Mondays to Fridays and 10:00am on Saturdays and Sundays. Closing time is at 10pm throughout the week.

+ Live music starts playing at 7:30pm onwards.

5. Bulgaden Castle Gastro Pub – the castle started out as a tavern in the 1700s and was then converted into a

restaurant in 1887. The castle holds several facilities that are each used for a different purpose. There are wedding venues, conference halls, and function rooms for intimate family gatherings. The Gastro Pub is where the new owners are trying to establish itself as local favorites.

They have recently launched the pub as a new and improved version of the castle's restaurant. The new menu contains a mix of local and international cuisines. Not only that, diners also get to enjoy the great view of the Ballyhoura Mountains while having enjoying some chitchat with their friends or loved ones.

Opening hours:

- The Gastro Pub opens at 12noon to 4:00pm on Mondays to Thursdays; 12noon to 8:00pm on Fridays and Saturdays; 12noon to 6:00pm on Sundays

Where to Stay

1. The Savoy – retreat to the luxurious Savoy Hotel after spending a day gallivanting around Limerick and exploring its museums. It is located on Henry Street, right at the heart of the city center. The hotels amenities include complementary newspapers, work desks, iron and ironing boards, and turndown service. These amenities are provided on all room types.

   The Savoy also has a restaurant, a tea room, and 2 different bars so that guests no longer have to go far to eat or to relax with a drink. Guests can also take advantage of the hotel's Ayurveda therapy for some holistic health care or they can just enjoy a simple Thai massage.

   Opening hours:

+ For information on check-in and check-out times, just call 35361448700. Or you can also send an email to reservations@savoylimerick.com to book a room.

2. Adare Camping, Caravan, and Motorhome Park – this 2-hectare park is approximately 35 minutes away from Lough Gur. It is a popular site for travellers who prefer to camp out while visiting Limerick. It is also a great option for tourists who are travelling with pets since pets are often not allowed in hotels and motels. There is enough room in the campsite for dogs and kids to run free, so that would break the monotony of sitting around in the car all day exploring the countryside.

The camp's facilities include a camper's kitchen, a laundry and ironing area, a ball playing field, shower stalls, and gas cylinders. Guests can also request for a hot tub at any point during their stay. The camp site is also located near the quaint village of Adare, which is just a 5-minute walk away. Guests can head over to the village to explore and to visit the only bank in the area.

Opening hours:

+ The campsite is only open from the 24th of March to the 11th of October. It's closed for the rest of the year.

3. Woodfield House Hotel – this hotel is located at the fringe of Limerick's city centre. As such, it is a gateway between two worlds: the urban sprawl of the city and the tree-lined greenery of the surrounding countryside. It can serve as a good base for those who want to go on daytime adventures in the wild but would still want to spend the night near the city. The hotel is fully-equipped with security features, specifically surveillance cameras around the private parking lot.

Other hotel amenities include newspapers by request at the reception, free wifi service, trouser pressing service, and a lot more. The restaurant also has a bar that has daily food service.

Opening hours:

- The bar serves food at 12noon to 3:30pm and 5:30pm to 8:30pm every day.

- For information on check-in and check-out times and other inquiries, contact 061 453 022 or send an email to woodfieldhotel@eircom.net.

4. Adare Manor Hotel and Golf Resort – this is a Neo-Gothic manor house that has been standing since the 1850s and served as the home of the Dunraven family. The manor house is steeped in mystery thanks to the 2nd Earl of Dunraven's eclectic tastes. In fact, his taste was so diverse that the manor remained unfinished upon his death. His son, the 3rd Earl of Dunraven, had to come home from England to take over the construction.

The Dunraven's retained ownership of the manor until 1982, after which it was sold to its current owners. No changes have been made to the manor house at all as a means of honoring its history. The manor house now has rooms and suites for in-house guests, as well as villas that are rented out as self-catering apartments. It sits on 840 acres of land. Guests can take a leisurely stroll of the well-tended garden and take souvenir photos on top of the bridge that lies at one side of the house.

Opening hours:

- Note that some parts of the manor house have been closed off for repairs. It is best to contact 1-800-462-3273 to verify room availability. The same number can be contacted for booking information, as well as check-in and check-out times.

5. Deebert House Hotel – this hotel is approximately 13 kilometers from the Ballyhoura Mountains, which should take about 29 minutes of travel time through the R512. It was built on the site of the old Deebert House mill that operated in the area since the 1800s. A crest of one of the mill's former owners has managed to survive and is now proudly displayed over the hotel's entrance gate.

The hotel can serve as a good base for those who wish to explore Kilmallock and Ballyhoura Mountain Trail. The hotel has taken the necessary steps to ensure the comfort of guests who love outdoor activities. They can dry off at the hotel's drying room and leave their bikes for safekeeping at the storage facility.

Opening hours:

⬥ Send an email to info@deeberthousehotel.com or call 063- 31200 for inquiries.

Nightlife in Limerick

Limerick's nightlife is as vibrant as in any other major city around Ireland. There are pubs and clubs everywhere, each with its own brand of clientele. There are certain bars that have become the favorite haunts of university students. These include the Smyths Bar and Icon Nightclub on Denmark Street, The Hurlers near the University of Limerick, and The Angel and The Office also on Denmark Street. These places draw the young crowd in mostly because of they have live bands that play this generation's brand of music.

The establishments also have cheaper entrance fees, with some bars offering free admission on occasion. There are also youth-oriented themes such as beach parties, foam parties, UV parties, and a lot of other wild ideas. But the most notable among these establishments is The Lodge. In fact, some students visit it more often than they to their classrooms for lessons. Regardless of where the party started, it always seems to end up at The Lodge.

Limerick also has a lot to offer the more mature party-goers. There are bars for those who want to have a quiet evening out. Those who want to go dancing can have their pick of the dance clubs. Those who want to enjoy some grunge music can also have their pick of grunge bars. There are pubs that are dedicated to traditional Irish entertainment and pubs that have nothing on the walls except sports stuff, specifically rugby.

Some of the most-recommended pubs for people aged 25 and above include:

- ✓ Dolans Pub on Dock Road

- ✓ The Old Quarter on the corner of Ellen and Denmark streets

- ✓ Michael Flannery Pub

They can also choose to visit any of the student's haunts if they wish to feel invigorated by the energy of the younger generation.

Chapter 6 Galway

Galway ranks on the fourth spot of Ireland's list of populous urban areas. It had a total population count of 76, 778 as of 2011. The city that is now Galway used to be a small settlement on the banks of the *Gaillimh* River, which is now known as the River Corrib. The King of Connacht and High King of Ireland, Tairrdelbach Ua Concobair ordered the establishment of the fort known as the *Dún Bhun na Gaillimhe* in 1124.

The fort eventually grew into a walled city that incorporated the small settlement that grew around it. Traces of these walls can still be seen around modern-day Galway. The Normans invaded in the early 13th century. Unlike other areas of Ireland where the invaders dominated the culture, the Norman invaders of Galway were the ones who assimilated. They were Gailicised, which means that they gained the characteristics of resident Gaels and shed most of their own Norman ways.

Galway was ruled by 14 merchant families from the mid-13th to the late 19th century. These families were known as the Tribes of Galway. Only 2 among these families were from native Irish origin, the rest were a mixture of Normans, Welsh, English, French, and Hiberno-Norman origins. The power that these families held over the city was disrupted now and then by several wars. It finally ended with the potato famine of the mid- 1800s.

Culture

Today, Galway is a city that has managed to skillfully combine the remnants of the past with the vibrant energy of modern times. It has a bohemian atmosphere complete with bright colors, loud music, and wild parties. Galway is also the only Irish city where Gaelic is still spoken freely in everyday conversation. In fact, the city has five divisions that are considered as Gaeltacht areas. These are areas where Irish is the predominantly-spoken language though the locals are well-versed in English.

Gaelic culture also thrives in the city with the abundance of Gaelic songs, music, and dance.

Where to Go

1. Hall of the Red Earl – this was once an august hall where Richard de Burgo, the Red Earl, ruled over the land in the 13th century. It is located right at the heart of the city and is one of Galway's major attractions. In its heyday, the castle served many purposes such as a custom's house, a courthouse, and a tax office. The castle fell into ruin when the De Burgo family was driven out of Galway by the Tribesmen.

   The castle's remains were unearthed in 1997 along with thousands of artefacts from the medieval period. Replicas of these are now on display and the castle itself has been placed has been placed under the protection of the *Dúchas na Gaillimhe* or the Galway Civic Trust.

   Opening hours:

   ✦ The castle is open for public viewing from Mondays to Fridays 9:30am to 6:45 pm.

   ✦ It is open for viewing on Saturdays 10:00am to 1:00pm on the months of May to September only.

   Where to go next: The Galway City Museum is a 2-minute walk away along the banks of the River Corrib.

2. Aran Islands or *Oileáin Árann* in Irish – the three islands that make up the Aran Islands are part of County Galway's Gaeltacht community. This means that even though the locals are quite fluent in English, they still converse mainly in Irish. Each of the islands is aptly named in Irish according to its size: Inis Mór –

the largest island, Inis Meàin –the mid-sized island, and Inis Oírr – the smallest island.

The islands are teeming with evidence of ancient Irish settlements. The most obvious evidence of its history are the forts at the cliff tops of the two largest islands, called Dún Aonghasa and Dún Chonchúir respectively. Inis Mór also has a number of Celtic monuments and ancient churches scattered about. The best way to explore the island is by hiring a bicycle from any of the stores that cater to tourists. You can bike around the island to its scenic spots and bring some food for a picnic along the edge of the cliffs.

Note that cars are rare in the islands since the people there travel by bike, in a horse and carriage, or on foot. A small minivan may be hired from the local tourist office but not many visitors choose this option as it ends the tour too quickly. People go to the islands to get away from the noise of the city and to engage in activities like swimming, snorkeling, canoeing, diving, bird watching and a lot more. They also get to immerse in authentic Irish culture that has remained slightly unchanged through the centuries.

Opening hours:

- The Aran Islands are open to visitors for most of the year. Your schedule would have to depend on the schedule of the ferry service from the mainland to the Inis Mór. Some ferries leave for Inis Mór at 10am and return to the mainland at 5pm. It may be possible to make arrangements for a different schedule but check with the tour operator for this. There are a number of accommodations around the islands for those who want to stay the night.

Where to go next: Explore the Connemara district.

3. Connemara District – the Connemara district lies along the western edge of Lough Corrib (Lake Corrib). The lake is connected to the sea through the River Corrib that dissects through the city of Galway. The district has a lot to offer tourists who want to immerse themselves in the wild beauty of the Irish coast. The Connemara derived its name from the tribal name *Conmacne Mara*, or the *Conmacne* tribe of the sea.

The district's most visible gem is the Twelve Bens (Irish: *Na Beanna Beola*) mountain range. The range consists of twelve small peaks that can be hiked within a day by dedicated climbers. Even novice climbers can breach most of the peaks of the Twelve Bens without difficulty since the trails are quite safe.

Aside from a hike to the Twelve Bens, visitors can also take hiking tours to explore the rest of the district. There are hidden gems everywhere. The walking tours will take them past megalithic tombs, amazing white-sand beaches, shimmering lakes that are as black as the night, boglands, and a whole lot more. If walking is too tiring, then you can also hire a bike from any of the shops that are scattered about the district.

Explore the Connemara Heritage and History Centre and the Connemara National Park. Take instagram-worthy photos at the Glorious Connemara Cycle amd go fishing Lough Mask.

Opening hours:

- The district can be explored at any time. It is best for those who are unfamiliar with the terrain to do their exploration in the daytime for safety purposes. Guided walks are provided by various tour companies. They should know the opening and closing hours of the various establishments along the way.

Where to go next: Head out across the river to County Mayo and climb the Mweelrea mountains. The view from the top includes the Twelve Bens on one side, a magnificent glaciated valley on another side, and the Atlantic as far as the eye can see.

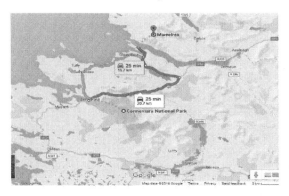

https://www.google.com.ph/maps/dir/Connemara+National+P ark,+Letterfrack,+Co.+Galway,+Ireland/Mweelrea,+Co.+Mayo, +Ireland

4. The Burren (*Boíreann*) National Park – at first look, it may not be obvious to visitors why the Burren is considered a national park. But once they absorb the beauty and majesty of the place, they will begin to understand why it the UNESCO awarded it as a Global Geopark. The park's size is approximately 1500 hectares and encompasses the famous Moher Cliffs.

Technically, the Burren is not part of Galway City since it is located in County Clare. But travel time from Galway is only just one hour by private car and the park is located just a few kilometres from the border between the two counties. It can also be reached via Limerick. Either way, the Burren is one part of Ireland that you really shouldn't miss out on if you have the chance to visit it.

Despite the fact that the Burren's landscape consists mostly of Limestone pavement, many plant species still thrives in it. The diversity of these species is attested to by the presence of plants from three different habitats: Arctic, Alpine, and Mediterranean. 23 native Irish orchids also grow in abundance on the park. Aside from marvelling at the amazing flora and fauna of the park, visitors can also climb up to the park's highest point: Knockanes.

But the park's crowning glory is the Cliffs of Moher. These majestic cliffs rise 200 metres up from the sea and encompass a total area of more than 8 kilometers. Avid moviegoers may have already seen a glimpse of these cliffs from popular movies including Harry Potter and the Half Blood Prince and The Princess Bride. The cliffs may not have been so obvious in Harry Potter since the movie only used footage of the entrance to a sea cave at the bottom of the cliff. Note to Pottermores: that's the cave where Voldemort hid one of the Horcruxes.

Opening hours:

- The Burren National Park is open to visitors throughout the year.

Where to go next: Explore the seaside town of Kinvarra, where the next item on this list is located.

5. Dunguaire Castle – this is a solitary castle that stands along the shores of Galway Bay. The castle's solitude is even more apparent when viewed at sunset after the daily throng of visitors have left and the bay is peaceful. If you're lucky, a swan may come flying in to provide the perfect complement to a photo of the sunset.

The castle was erected in the early 16th century. It is believed that the castle was built on the same site as the palace of King Guaire of Connacht. Visitors to the castle are treated to a medieval banquet complete with costumed servers and medieval forms of entertainment.

Opening hours:

- The castle is only open during the months of April to October. Day tours are available from 10:00am to 5:00pm. Those who wish to partake of the nightly banquet have to book a reservation first. The banquet is at 5:30pm and 8:45pm.

Where to go next: Head back to the city and explore Galway on foot. Walking tours can be booked with some of Galway's best-known guides. These would take you around some of the most historic parts of the city, including many of its medieval buildings.

Side trip: Drive off for about an hour and a half from Galway City to Lough Key Forest Park in County Roscommon. The park is popular for its lake that contains numerous little islands. Most of these islands bear some historical significance. The most significant among these islands is the one known as Castle Island, or the Rock. It was once home to the mighty McDermotts, Kings of Moylurg.

There is so much more to learn about and explore in Lough Key, so be sure reserve some time on your itinerary.

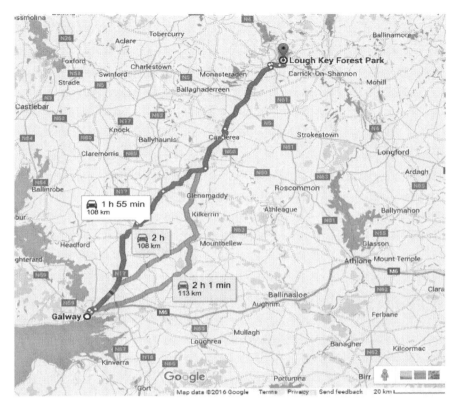

https://www.google.com.ph/maps/dir/Galway,+Ireland/Lough+Key+F orest+Park,+Boyle,+Co.+Roscommon,+Ireland

Where to Eat

1. Druid Lane Restaurant and Wine Bar – the restaurant has been operating for more than a decade now. What makes it special is the fact that it is located in a building that has historic value. The building was erected in 1663 under the orders of King Charles II. He leased it out to the George Monck, the 1st Duke of Albermarle. The proprietors have taken care to ensure that the building's old world charm remains intact.

   Druid Lane's menu includes a wide selection of native Irish dishes that include seafood and selected meat recipes. Guests are also going to love the ambience inside the restaurant with its colorful walls and candle lights hung from most corners.

Another thing that adds to the Druid Lane's charm is the fact that it is located in Galway's most vibrant area: the Latin Quarter. Visitors can stroll along its medieval-inspired streets to enjoy the view of the quaint shops and cafes. They might even find a knickknack or two to bring back home.

Opening hours:

+ Druid Lane serves dinner daily from 4pm to midnight.

2. Tigh Ruairi –this is one of the leading restaurants in Inis Oírr and locals also refer to it as Rory's. The establishment has been around since the 19th century though it went by a different name. Guests can also check in to one of its quaint rooms to the night. Tigh Ruairi has retained its traditional Irish vibe with music, food, and drinks that bring guests back to the early years.

Opening hours:

+ Tigh Ruairi is a bed and breakfast place that is open for visitors at any time.

3. Tigh Giblin Pub, Restaurant, and Music Venue – for tourists who have already eaten at Tigh Giblin, there's one thing about the place that certainly stuck in their minds: the fact that the menus are interspersed with English and Irish entries. For instance, starters are listed under Mar Thús, salad and herb selections are listed under Ón Ngarraí and so on.

Opening hours:

+ Mondays to Thursdays 11:30am to 11:30pm

+ Fridays to Saturdays 11:30am to 12:30pm

＋ Sundays 12noon to 11:30pm

4. Cullinan's Seafood Restaurant – this quaint restaurant is located in the town of Doolin. It is set amidst the rugged wildness of Ireland's coast facing the Atlantic Ocean. The menu consists mostly of traditional Irish dishes with all of its ingredients obtained from local sources. The restaurant has won several prestigious awards for the superior quality of its dishes.

There is also an extensive wine list filled with local and international wine brands.

Opening hours:

＋ Restaurant operations start on Easter and lasts until the weekend of bank holidays in October. Food is served from 6:00pm to 9:00pm daily on these months, except for Wednesdays and Saturdays when the restaurant is closed. Guests are advised to make a prior reservation.

5. Morans Oyster Cottage – this restaurant takes its oyster supply from the Clarenbridge Oyster bed. The 700-acre oyster bed lies along the mouth of two rivers: Clarenbridge and Dunkellin. It is a favorite hunting ground among locals who love to feast on oysters every now and then.

Aside from its sumptuous oyster recipes, Morans Oyster Cottage also offers a wide variety of seafood dishes. These include clams steamed in wine and traces of garlic, seafood chowder, garlic mussels, and a lot more. The establishment also has some historic importance as it has been standing on the same spot for over 200 years. It is also owned by the same family that established it 2 centuries ago, the Moran family of County Galway.

Morans Oyster Cottage has a homey feel and provides an amazing view of the sea. It is a welcome retreat for tourists who have just absorbed the almost depressing solitude of Dunguaire Castle.

Opening Hours:

- ⚜ Food is served at lunchtime from 12noon to 11:30pm Mondays to Thursdays.

- ⚜ The restaurant closes at midnight on Fridays and Saturdays.

- ⚜ The restaurant closes two and a half hours early on Sundays, at 9:30pm.

Where to Stay

1. The House Hotel – this hotel is just a one-minute walk away from the Hall of the Red Earl. It is a 4-star hotel that offers standard, deluxe, and super deluxe rooms, as well as house suites. It is also located at the colourful Latin Quarter, so guests should have no shortage of fun and exciting new experiences. The hotel also has a restaurant that serves food and wine in the evenings.

   The hotel's amenities include discounted parking rates, complimentary newspaper on all rooms, electronic safety deposit boxes, and a few other things that depend on the type of room that you book.

   Opening hours:

   - ⚜ Call 091 538900 or send an email to info@thehousehotel.ie for inquiries on opening hours and room rates/availability.

2. Tig Congaile B&B – this is located in Inis Meain, the middle island of the Aran Islands. There are many other accommodations that are scattered about the three islands. But this one was chosen because it provides a stunning view of the Cliffs of Moher, which lies across the sea from the island. Spending a night at the inn can

be a balm to any soul, as there is no other sound except for the ones created by nature.

Tig Congaile also has a restaurant that serves an eclectic mix of dishes. These dishes have a Latin American taste thanks mostly to the inn's Guatemalan chef. But there are also a variety of traditional Irish dishes to be enjoyed.

Opening hours:

- Call the proprietor at (+353) 09973085 or send an email to bbinismeain@gmail.com for inquiries.

3. Abbeyglen Castle – this is the perfect place to stay for people who want to feel like royalty even for just a few nights. Abbeyglen Castle Hotel is located in Clifden, Connemara, at the foot of the famous Twelve Bens. It is a perfect starting point for those who want to go on a walking tour of Twelve Bens and the surrounding countryside.

Guests who book via the castle-hotel's website are entitled to special privileges. These include complimentary champagne upon their arrival, free tickets to the Connemara National Park, Free parking and wifi, and free admission tickets to Kylemore Abbey.

Opening hours:

- The castle accepts new check-ins from 8:00am to 11:00pm daily.

4. Aran View Country House – as the name of the establishment suggests, it is located on a spot that provides a great view of the Aran Islands. The Aran View has several bedrooms to accommodate guests, as well 2 cottages that serve as self-catering accommodations. Those who are in the area to explore

the Burren and the Aran Islands can make the Aran View Country House as their base.

The Aran View stands on 100 acres of fertile farmland, which means that guests would have enough privacy to roam around and enjoy the view. This is perfect for honeymooners and tourists who are seeking some alone time. Some of the establishment's facilities include the following in each room:

> TV

> Private Bathrooms

> A phone with access to local and international calls

The self-catering accommodations also have separate kitchen and dining areas, private parking space, complete toiletries, and complete kitchen necessities. This is a good place for families to leave their car before leaving for the Aran Islands. After all, they won't be able to bring it with them on the ferries anyway.

Opening hours:

+ Call the proprietor at +353 65 707 4061 or send an email to info@aranview.com for inquiries.

5. Kinvara Guesthouse – this is a 4-star bed and breakfast place that's just 3 mins away from Dunguaire Castle. It is also just 53 minutes away from the Burren. There's a lot of beauty to explore in the area, which makes Kinvara Guesthouse a great starting point. The rooms are also comfortable enough to make it a great place to come home to after a tiring day of adventures.

Kinvara's facilities include a flat-screen TV on each of the 23 bedrooms, en suite bathrooms, and free WIFI service. Guests are also provided with complete toiletries. There is on-site parking as well.

Opening hours:

- Call the proprietor at +353 91 638562 or send an email to kinvaraguesthouse@gmail.com for inquiries.

Nightlife in Galway

Galway's nightlife is popular for the way that it mixes the city's current modern vibe with its past of being a small town. Decades-old drinking pubs that still display most of its old furnishings lie side by side with some of the newest clubs that contain the newest entertainment system in the city. Tourists can choose to enjoy a tall Irish pint while enjoying some traditional Irish music. Or they can also choose to gyrate mindlessly to the music of the new generation while taking small sips of strong drinks with international brands.

For those who do not know exactly where to go, traditional music can be had at any of the following venues:

- ✓ Monroe's Tavern
- ✓ Pucan
- ✓ Roisin Dubh
- ✓ The Galway Shawl
- ✓ Tigh Neachtain

Of course, that's not to mention the traditional Irish restaurants that are already previously mentioned in other sections of this chapter. But since Galway is a semi-Gaeltacht city, it is entirely possible that the people who frequent these establishments may converse in Irish. The menus and signs may also be written in Irish as well. Understandably, these may cause some confusion in an inebriated tourist's mind.

Those who wish to stick with popular music can go to any other nightclub or bar that's scattered around the city. The Front Door Pub in the Latin Quarter is popular among the twenty-something crowd. The pub has a live band and a DJ from Mondays to Wednesdays. Closing time is usually around 2 in the morning. Other popular hangouts for this type of crowd include The King's Head, Halo, Coyotes Late Bar, The Skeff, and Karma.

For those who wish to have a conversation while enjoying their drinks, they best head out to the Dàil Bar on the corner of Middle Street and Cross Street. This is a favorite meeting place for locals where they can be free to discuss the events of the day. In fact, the bar's name, Dàil, is an Irish word that literally means 'meeting place'.

Chapter 6 Waterford

Waterford is the oldest city in all of Ireland, having been around for over 1100 years. In fact, unlike the names of the other Irish cities, Waterford does not have an Irish equivalent. But it does have a Viking name: *vedrarfjord*. The Vikings and the native Irish fought for control of the port city from 853 to 917. The Vikings finally won out and subsequently ruled the area until the Norman invasion in 1171.

In medieval times, Waterford ranked second to Dublin in prominence. It was a favorite of the British Crown. Waterford maintained is Catholic city status despite pressure from Britain to convert to Protestantism. A Catholic government ruled the city betweek 1642 and 1649 until it was retaken by the Cromwells in 1650.

Waterford prospered in the 1700s with numerous architectural wonders being built throughout the city. The British also built Martello towers in 1800s to protect the city. The British military presence in the city was also strengthened.

Culture

Living in the oldest city in all of Ireland is something that the residents of Waterford do not take lightly. Almost every person is aware if his or her genealogy and the role that his or her family played at some point in Waterford's past. The city's museums and information centers are all focused on providing visitors with detailed chronicles of Waterford's historic past. But this is not to say that the city is stuck in the past.

The people are also quite focused on the present. This is apparent in the constant discussion of the latest sports scores in pubs and bars around the city. Just like any other Irish city, Waterford is also hooked on football. Its official team is the Waterford United F.C., which is headquartered at the Waterford Regional Sports Centre.

In terms of language, English is primarily spoken by 99% of Waterford's residents. But as in all the other Irish cities, official signs are written both in English and Gaelic. There is a tiny Gaeltacht community along the coast to the west of Dungarvan. Despite the fact that Waterford is not a Gaeltacht city, visitors may have a little trouble understanding the locals at first. That's because through the years, the locals have developed a slang that contains an extensive vocabulary.

This slang primarily consists of English words and phrases though it may be interspersed with a sprinkling of Irish words. Tourists who truly wish to immerse themselves in the culture of Waterford can go to UpTheDeise.com for a rough translation of many slang words and phrases. They may also be able to pick up a few local jokes on the site that could come in handy during drinking sessions with the locals.

Where to Go

1. House of Waterford Crystal – Waterford Crystal is well-known throughout the world for its unique brilliance and intricate designs. The quality of the lead crystal used on Waterford Crystal makes it a leading choice for commemorative pieces. These pieces are still carefully hand-crafted at the House of Waterford Crystal, even though it is no longer an Irish-owned company.

   A trip to the House of Waterford Crystal should satisfy the curiosity of any tourist who is attracted to glittering things. The establishment has a vast selection of truly expensive genuine Waterford Crystal pieces on display at the Retail Store. Aside from gawking at the brilliant display, visitors are also given a tour of the factory. They get to witness first-hand how the House of Waterford's craftsmen blow, mould, hand-mark, cut, sculpt, and engrave the crystal pieces.

   Tickets can be purchased online at www.waterfordvisitorcentre.com/cart for 10%less than the door price. Adults are charged at €12.15 per head and children 5 to 18 years old are charged at €4.00 per individual. Families can choose to pay the bulk ticket price of €30.00 for 2 adults and 2 children.

Opening hours:

Note that the Factory Tour and the Retail have separate opening times that also vary according to the month. The schedule is as follows:

- Factory Tour:

    o January to February: 9:30am to 3:15pm Mondays to Fridays

    o March: 9:00am to 3:15pm Mondays to Saturdays and 9:30am to 3:15pm on Sundays.

    o April to October (except October 31st): 9:00am to 4:15pm Mondays to Saturdays and 9:30am to 4;15pm on Sundays.

    o November to December: 9:30am to 3:15pm Mondays to Fridays

- Retail Store:

    o January to February: 9:30am to 5:00pm Mondays to Saturdays.

    o March: 9:00am to 5:00pm Mondays to Saturdays and 9:30am to 5:00pm on Sundays.

    o April to October: 9:00am to 6:00pm Mondays to Saturdays and 9:30am to 6:00pm on Sundays.

- November to December: 9:30am to 5:00pm Mondays to Saturdays and 12:00noon to 5:00pm on Sundays.

- Note that both establishments are closed on St Patrick's Day, March 17th.

Where to go next: Spend a few relaxing hours at the People's park, which is just 5 minutes away.

2. Waterford's Museums – there are three museums located in the Viking Triangle of the city. These are:

   a. Reginald's Tower – this civic building is the oldest of its kind all of Ireland. The Vikings first built a tower on the site in 914, which then served as the apex of the Viking settlement that developed in a triangular fashion. The ruins of this old tower were gradually rebuilt between the 12th and the 15th centuries by the Anglo-Normans.

   The tower is now considered as the center of Waterford's Viking history. It holds bulk of the artifacts that were found on archaeological digs around the River Suir.

   b. The Medieval Museum – this museum is dedicated solely towards the history of Waterford during medieval times. It holds many of the important documents of that time, such as the Great Charter Roll. The roll is at least 4-meters long and contains a depiction of the medieval city of Waterford. It also has depictions of 5 medieval English kings, the king's deputies that were stationed in Ireland, and the mayors. The document is unique not only Ireland but also in England.

   Aside from the Great Charter Roll, the Medieval Museum also houses two chambers of medieval history: the Chorister's Hall of the 13th century and the Mayor's Wine Vault of the 15th century.

c. The Bishop's Palace – this building has always been admired as an exquisite piece of architecture from the moment it was built until today. It also completes the 1000-year time-travel of Waterford's museums. That's because it holds historic pieces that encompass the years between the 1700s to the 1970s. The collection includes the oldest known piece of Waterford crystal, referred to as the Penrose decanter. The last surviving piece of 'mourning cross' that commemorated Napoleon Bonaparte's death is also housed in the Palace.

Opening hours:

+ Reginald's Tower is open from 9:30am to 5:00pm on Wednesdays to Sundays from January to the first half of March. It closes at 5:30pm on the same days from the second half of March to Mid-December. It is closed from the 24th December to the 6th of January.

+ The Medieval Museum

Where to go next: Head over to the tiny fishing village of Dunmore East along the western portion of Waterford Harbour. The village's history dates back to the time of the Vikings, which means that it has plenty for history buffs to see.

3. The Copper Coast – this was officially declared as a Geopark by the UNESCO in 2004 due to its important contribution to Waterford's geologic history. It encompasses 90 kilometers of Waterford's coastline stretching from Fenor to Stradbally. You definitely have to sign up for a walking tour of the Geopark because there is so much to do and to see at the site. Note that geoparks are places that make use of the natural

geologic features and heritage of the area for ecotourism.

The Copper Coast got its name from the copper mines that used to operate in the area from 1825 to its slow decline in the 1850s and subsequent closure in 1880. Copper was not the only mineral mined since there were also rich deposits of lead and silver. Some remnants of the mines still remain in Tankardstown and Bunmahon. Tourists can go on a virtual tour of the mines too.

Other activities that can be enjoyed at the Copper Coast include exploring the different beaches that form part of the park. Different water sports activities can also be enjoyed in these beaches including diving, angling, and kayaking. The last one is the best way to access some of the caves along the coastline. The park also includes a vast tract of land where tourists can go on picnics amidst the bogs of Fenor or in the Ballymoat Gardens of Dunhill or the Littlewood Gardens of Stradbally.

Opening Hours:

- The park is closed during the Irish winter. The park is open mostly the weekends during the summer months. However, since the park is operated mostly by volunteers, it may sometimes be short-staffed. This means that it would also be closed. That's why it's highly-recommended to call +353 (0)51 292828 first so that a visit can be arranged at the most convenient schedule.

Where to go next: Explore the old railway line, which is the next item on this list.

4. Waterford and Suir Valley Railway – this railway line is now listed on Ireland's Heritage Railways list. It was established in 1872 and had the distinction of being the most expensive railway line of its time. While the

railway was operational, it had stations on several villages including:

a. Carroll's Cross (was only added in 1882)

b. Cappagh

c. Cappoquin

d. Dungarvan

e. Durrow and Stradbally

f. Kilmeadan

g. Kilmacthomas

h. Lismore

Closure of the railway line started in a gradual process until finally, the last train hooted to a stop in 1987. That was the last commercial journey on the Waterford-Dungarvan railway line. Today, this line is now used on tours of the glorious old railway line. Visitors get to ride on open carriages that take them to some of the most picturesque spots in Kilmeadan and its surrounds. Some of these sites, such as Mount Congreve Gardens, cannot be accessed through any other means except by train.

Opening hours:

- The railway line is only open during the summer months. Train schedules are as follows:

  o May to August: One-hour intervals beginning at 11:00am to 4:00pm on Mondays to Saturdays. One-hour intervals beginning at 12noon to 5:00pm on Sundays.

  o September: One-hour intervals beginning at 11:00am to 3:00pm on Mondays to

Saturdays. One-hour intervals beginning at 12noon to 4:00pm on Sundays.

Where to go next: The railway should take you straight to the Davitts Quay Opp Pub train station in Dungarvan. Disembark on that station and spend a day or two exploring the town of Dungarvan on a walking or biking tour. This coastal town used to be the central town of County Waterford before it merged with the Waterford City Council. About 3% of the town's population speak Irish in daily conversation outside of the schoolroom. Don't forget to visit Dungarvan Castle and Devonshire Bridge while you're there.

5. Lismore or *Lios Mór* in Irish – this is an ancient town on the banks of the River Blackwater. The town has been around since the time of Saint Carthage, whose Irish name was *Mo Chutu Mac Fínaill*. The town has several historic sites and buildings that date back to hundreds of years ago. As such, it is now considered as one of Ireland's heritage towns.

Some of its popular historic buildings include the Lismore Castle and the Lismore Cathedral. Lismore Castle was erected in 1185 through the orders of Prince John. The castle was built on the same site where the revered monastery, Lismore Abbey, used to stand. The Abbey was founded by St Carthage in 635, two years before his untimely death.

Lismore Castle initially served as the official residence of Lismore's bishops. It changed ownership several times and was at one point bought by Sir Walter Raleigh. The Dukes of Devonshire has owned the castle from the early 18th century to the present day. It is currently being leased out to interested parties, though the current Duke's heir still maintains a private apartment within the castle.

Admission to the castle and gardens is charged at €8.00 per adult. Seniors, children and students are charged at €5.00 each. Families with 2 adults and 3 children can choose the family ticket price of €20.00

Lismore Cathedral is also another historic building that has been standing since medieval times. It was destroyed and repaired several times.

Opening hours:

+ The main gallery and the gardens of the Lismore Castle are open to visitors from the 25th of March to the 30th of September this year (2016). It opens at 10:30am and closes at 5:30pm from Mondays to Sundays. Last admission is at 4:30pm.

+ The Lismore Cathedral is open to visitors as well as to people who would like to attend mass services. Visitors can gain entry at 9:00am all year round. The cathedral closes its doors to visitors at 6:00pm from April to September and at 4:00pm from October to March. Mass hours are normally at 8:00am every first and third Sunday of the month. There is also a service at 11:30am every Sunday.

Where to go next: Book a tour of the River Blackwater cruise. The starting point of the cruise is in the heritage town of Youghal in County Cork. The boat then follows the river northward until it reaches its final destination in County Kerry. The route takes you to some of the most picturesque views along the River Blackwater. This includes some sites that are not accessible through walking or biking tours.

Side Trip: The Rock of Cashel (*Carraig Phádraig*) in County Tipperary. It is also referred to in formal conversation as St. Patrick's Rock and most locals refer to it as the Cashel of Kings. These two names are inferences to the widespread belief that the Great King Aenghus of Munster was converted to Christianity on that rock by no other than St. Patrick himself. The event happened sometime around the 5th century AD. You have to go see it in order to believe that truly complex mix of architectural beauty can exist.

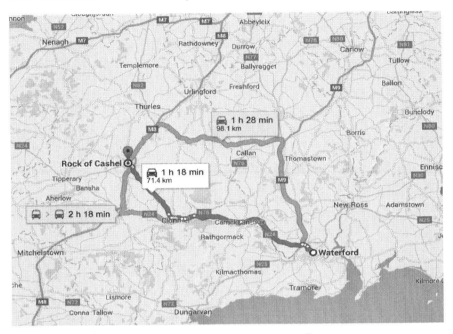

https://www.google.com.ph/maps/dir/Waterford,+Ireland/Rock+of+Ca shel,+Cashel,+Co.+Tipperary,+Ireland

Where to Eat

1. Crystal Cafe – when you're on a tour of the famous House of Waterford Crystal, there's no need to get out of the premises just to grab a bite. The Crystal Cafe serves sumptuous homemade snacks that are paired with premium Irish coffee.

   Opening hours:

   ♣ The cafe normally follows the same schedule as the rest of the House of Waterford Crystal.

2. La Boheme Restaurant – this fancy restaurant serves authentic French cuisine prepared by a genuine French chef. He also happens to be the establishment's owner. The restaurant is located in a restored Georgian building that adds to the overall bohemian vibe of the place. This vibe is completed by arched ceilings and candles lit on each table with a candelabra on the mantel.

Just like many of Ireland's leading restaurants, all of La Boheme's ingredients are obtained from local suppliers, artisans, farmers, and producers. This method of buying local ensures the freshness of the ingredients, which add to the natural flavor of the final dish. Despite its dedication to French cuisine, La Boheme also serves authentic locally-crafted Irish beer.

Opening hours:

- La Boheme opens for dinner starting at 5:30pm until late on Mondays to Saturdays.

- Lunch is served on Fridays and the restaurant is also open on Sundays and Bank Holidays.

3. The Copper Hen – this casual dining restaurant is located in a village called Fenor on the Copper Coast, which is where it got its name. It is a relatively new establishment since operation started in 2010. But that doesn't mean that it doesn't have anything to boast of yet. The Copper Hen has already taken home several awards in its short tenure in its relatively short tenure.

The Copper Hen's menu includes dishes that are fun to eat but wouldn't take off a huge chunk of a tourist's budget. The ingredients are all locally-sourced to ensure freshness and fullness of flavor. Some of its critically-acclaimed menu items include fresh crab claws tossed in herbs and spices, Irish Hereford sirloin beef traditionally cooked, and a lot more.

Opening hours:

- The restaurant opens at dinnertime only on Wednesdays to Saturdays, and lunchtime only on Sundays.

4. Tannery Restaurant – the items on the Tannery's menu often change depending on which ingredients are currently in season. Visitors have 5 different menu types to choose from. The Chef's Table menu is popular among large groups of diners. That's because it consists of three different dishes that the entire group can pass around to each other. The idea behind this concept is that sharing the food or passing it around helps in creating a cordial atmosphere between the guests.

Opening hours:

- The Tannery opens for lunch on Fridays and Sundays at 12:30pm. It closes at 2:30pm on Fridays and 3:30pm on Sundays.

- The restaurant opens for dinner at 5:30pm on Tuesdays to Saturdays. It closes at 9:00pm on Tuesdays to Thursdays and at 9:30pm on Fridays and Saturdays.

- The Tannery is also open for dinner on the Sunday night before a bank holiday from 6:00pm to 9:00pm.

5. The Summer House – this is a quaint restaurant that is tucked away at the back of a homestore cum bakery. Most of the items on the menu are freshly-baked from the freshest ingredients. Some of these have slowly become the favorites among the local, such as the buttery croissants, and the decadent dark chocolate cakes. You can visit the restaurant to grab a quick bite of cake or to enjoy some home-cooked lunch and then order some takeaway for the journey home.

Opening hours:

- ⵌ The cafe serves tea or coffee and pastries from 10:00am to 5:30pm from Tuesdays to Sundays. It serves lunch at 12:30pm to 2:30pm on Tuesdays to Saturdays only.

Where to Stay

1. Cliff House Hotel – just as the name implies, this hotel is located right at the edge of a cliff that overlooks Ardmore Bay. Hotel guests can enjoy sumptuous meals on a terrace while enjoying the sound of the Atlantic pushing against the rocks below. The hotel also has a long history, having been established in the 1930s to cater to the gradually increasing wave of tourists visiting Ardmore Bay. It is 23 minutes away from the town of Youghal.

   The hotel provides guests with access to a wide variety of outdoor activities. These include whale watching, fly-fishing, day hikes (guided), horseback riding, and a lot more. Its facilities include everything that can be expected from a 5-star hotel.

   Opening hours:

   - ⵌ Contact the hotel's information desk at +353 24 87800 or send an email to info@thecliffhousehotel.com to inquire about check-in and check-out times.

2. The Coach House Hotel – this hotel used to serve as the coachhouse for the once-formidable Butlerstown Castle. The Castle's history dates back to ancient times, when it was still known as the Manor of Killotteran. The Blundestons were its first owners, who then passed it on to the Butlers (from whom the town's name was taken). Ownership of the castle passed on to several

hands throughout the centuries. It has also served an important purpose during the War of Independence.

After the war, the estate surrounding the castle was divided according to the provisions of the Land Act. The castle's last owners auctioned off most of its contents and they then moved to the coach house to live there. The Coach House has since been restored and now serves as a small hotel. Each of the hotel's rooms is furnished with traditional materials but is fully-equipped with modern amenities.

The amenities include free wifi service, direct dial phone service, a TV, and tea or coffee-making facilities. The hotel's charm lies in the fact that it is located in a town where the nearest neighbors are miles away. This means that guests can expect a good night's sleep in the quiet of their bedrooms. But Waterford City is also just 15 minutes away, so they can drive off to that direction anytime they need the noise of the urban jungle.

Opening hours:

+ The Coach House is open for business during the months of April to October only.

3. Athenaeum House Hotel – this hotel used to be the merchant house of the Whites, one of Waterford's leading shipbuilders in the early 1800s. The house itself has been standing since 1810. Although many parts of the house have undergone some necessary replacements, the current owners still managed to retain some of original parts. These include the plaster work in many parts of the hotel, the windows, and the fireplaces.

Athenaeum House is a great starting point for those who wish to explore the River Suir and its surrounds. In fact, the hotel is a good place to enjoy a great view of the River Suir at any time of the day. Most of the rooms are overlooking the River and the nearby Wateford Harbour.

The hotel's amenities include flatscreen TVs on each of the rooms, free wifi service, telephone with direct dialing access, tea and coffee-making facilities, and an iron and ironing board. Unlike other hotels where all the rooms are identical, the rooms at the Athenaeum House each have its own unique flair. No two rooms are decorated in the exact same manner, and guests can choose which rooms they feel most in tune with.

Opening hours:

- The hotel is open to guests throughout the year. But since they also provide the entire hotel for lease to large groups, it is best to contact them to inquire about room availability prior to booking. The contact number is +353 (0) 51-83 39 99 or send an email to info@athenaeumhousehotel.com.

4. Ard Na Ciúin – this place is a haven for holistic health enthusiasts. It is seemingly located in the middle of nowhere, though it can easily be reached via the N72. It is about an hour and a half's drive away from Waterford City and is only 15 minutes away from Lismore. The hotel/spa is located within a 15-acre farm where everything is grown in an organic manner, no fertilizers, pesticides, or anything like that.

Everything that's served in the hotel's restaurant is home-cooked and home-grown, including the livestock. The facilities include a unique endless pool that looks shorter that it actually is and a hydro-massage hot tub that can be adjusted to various settings. In-room amenities include TVs and DVD players for each room, fresh towels and linen, complimentary robe, complete toiletries, a hairdryer, a tea and coffee-making facility, and an iron and ironing board.

Opening hours:

- Call +353 58 60976 or send an email to info@ardnaciuin.ie for inquiries.

5. Lismore House Hotel – this is another one of the many establishments that the Duke of Devonshire built. The Duke had this built in 1797 with the actual purpose of using it as a hotel. The hotel's Georgian charm is still quite obvious both inside and outside of the building. The old-world charm of most of its original bedrooms clash nicely with modern fixtures of everyday life.

The hotel's amenities include plasma TVs with access to satellite channels, broadband internet connection, direct dial phone service, and tea and coffee-making facilities. Each room also has a hair dryer and an iron with an ironing board. Guests can also choose to have a newspaper delivered to their rooms during their stay.

Opening hours:

- Call +353 (0)58 72966 for inquiries.

Nightlife in Waterford

Waterford's nightlife is not only composed of drinking in nightclubs, pubs, and bars. Tourists can also visit the local theatres or watch a local Irish movie in any of the night-time cinemas. The Theatre Royal has shows that start at 8 or 9pm for the evening crowd to enjoy. For instance, you just might be able to catch the production of Marc Robert singing the music of John Denver on the 19th of March. Showing time for that one is 9pm.

The Theatre is filled with shows for the entire month. For tourists whose travel plans are still uncertain, they can always go to the theatre's website to see what's showing while they're in Waterford. The website address is www.theatreroyal.ie.

Another option for nighttime entertainment in Waterford is to watch the Greyhound racing at the Kilcohan Park Greyhound Stadium. The stadium is a fully-licensed racing track that strictly follows the guidelines set by the Irish Greyhound Board. Racing events normally occur on Fridays and Saturdays from 7pm onwards.

If you're neither interested in racing nor theatre, then the only other option left is to paint the town a deep shade of red with the help of the ever-reliable Irish whisky. There are many nightclubs and bars scattered throughout the city for every picky tourist's tastes. There are gay bars, comedy bars, dance clubs, and so on. You also have your pick pub houses that play modern and traditional Irish music, either live or recorded. Some of these establishments play traditional every single night of the week, while others follow a strict schedule.

T&H Doolans is one of the few places that play traditional music nightly.

Conclusion

Ireland is a small country that is steeped in history and folklore. Exploring its nooks and crannies should be an enjoyable experience because there really is something in the country for every type of tourist. If you are the kind of tourist who is hooked on castles and medieval architecture, then there should be a lot of that in every Irish city. If you prefer enjoying the great outdoors, then go on a biking tour of the entire country and enjoy the outdoors to your heart's content.

Most of the time, exploring the Irish countryside doesn't have to be done in an extravagant manner. Just do what the Irish do: hire a bike and pedal on to wherever that road may lead you. Sooner or later, you're bound to come across a view that's so beautiful that it makes all that pedaling well worth it. But don't go looking for leprechauns along the way, because that really is just part of the rich Irish mythology.

43810705R00051

Made in the USA
San Bernardino, CA
28 December 2016